Zeal Without Knowledge?

**A GUIDE FOR THE NEW BELIEVER AND
BABES IN CHRIST!**

Nikeya Quick

REJOICE
Essential Publishing

Zeal Without Knowledge?/Nikeya Quick

ISBN-13: 978-1-956775-81-5

TABLE OF CONTENTS

Acknowledgements

WOULD LIKE TO ACKNOWLEDGE Jesus Christ, my Lord and Savior, and God the Father, for being my firm foundation in this walk of life. I would also like to acknowledge my mother and father, Richard and Doris Miller, for their encouragement, prayers, and dedication as parents to me as I endeavor to be all that God has called me to be. Thank you for your wisdom and love.

Introduction

ZEAL WITHOUT KNOWLEDGE IS full of the keys of wisdom, understanding, and instruction. It is a book that will outline to the readers keys to help in their walk with Christ.

One of the pros of becoming "a Believer" and "being a member of the body of Christ," is the sacrifice you must make by taking up your cross and denying yourself just like Jesus did. The Bible says in *Matthew 16:24 NLT, "Then Jesus said to his disciples, If any of you wants to be my follower, you must give up your own way, take up your cross, and follow me."* In this walk, as you follow Jesus Christ, you will experience opposition and many other things that you are told about in the Word of God (the Bible).

There are issues that can cause a stumbling block or hinderance to your spiritual growth and development in your new walk with God through His Son, Jesus Christ.

The reason I consider following Jesus Christ by taking up your cross, and denying yourself daily a "pro" and not a "con," is because it produces good fruit in your life spiritually.

Your flesh will not like the change that the Lord is making in your life, but that's okay. You will become stronger spiritually as you grow and develop in Christ! Have you ever met someone who was excited and eager to take on a project or a task? As they began, they were positive, full of energy, raised their sleeves, and ready to get their hands dirty. When they started to do the project, they saw barriers that would hinder them from completing the project or assignment.

Barriers like not knowing what to expect after completing the initial step in the assignment would catch them off guard. When this happens, the person will immediately need to stop and regroup to find out how to get to the next phase of the project, focusing on the completion. So, they do some research in the manual for the project and read it thoroughly, but when they try to perform the next step, they must do it repeatedly until it is perfect.

No one wants to turn in a project that is mediocre or incomplete. Everyone always has a mission to complete the assignment. This is a blueprint of what it is like to become a believer and how to overcome barriers, temptations, weaknesses, and failures after you receive salvation.

Wisdom and understanding are necessary to achieve the goal and complete the race of salvation! That is eternal life with

God, the Father, and Jesus Christ, the Son of the Living God, and being a joint heir and heir in the kingdom of heaven.

This book will help you to recognize the booby traps and snares set by the enemy to hinder your God-given purpose and your right in the kingdom of heaven.

CHAPTER 1

Confidence and Self-esteem

YOU MUST KNOW WHO you are, what you were created for, and the area that God created and gifted you for. This is imperative because if you don't know who you are and your purpose here in the earth, anyone will be able to tell you what or who you are, and it may be contrary to the will of God, and we know that only he that does the will of the Father is he that will enter heaven (Matthew 7:21).

Do not condemn yourself for the bad decisions you have made in your past and for the things that have happened to you because you weren't alert and being simple. Proverbs is a great place to start if you lack wisdom in anything. If any man lacks wisdom, ask and God will give it to you (James 1:5).

Ask the Lord to show you who you are. Ask Him to reveal your identity and who He created you to be. Ask and it shall be given to you, knock and the door shall be open, seek and ye shall find (Matthew 7:7).

Every person's life has value. God didn't allow one person to be born into the world without His purpose and destiny placed on the inside of them (Genesis 1:26).

God is also a God of free will. He will give you a choice to choose Him or the life you want to live. This is where you choose between life and death (Deuteronomy 30:19).

Don't allow your focus to rest on what other people are doing or how they prosper. The Bible says the steps of a good man are ordered by the Lord and He delights in his way (Psalms 37:23). The Lord has already ordered your steps. He foreknew and predestined you to be conformed to the image of His Son, Jesus Christ. He called, justified, and glorified you (Romans 8:29-31).

WISDOM KEYS:

Don't allow people to speak to you disrespectfully. We train people on how to treat us by what we accept. If they don't treat you with respect and dignity, you need to move on, whether in a friendship or a heterosexual relationship.

Be capable of making decisions on your own, without another person's input and be content with your decisions. The Bible says a double minded man is unstable in all his ways (James 1:8).

Always put your listening ears on when you are interacting with people. I am not speaking about paranoia, but being sober and vigilant. Even the most eloquent speakers will give their motives and intentions concerning you through their speech. The difference between discernment is the feeling or the voice of God that rejects what is being presented to you. Paranoia causes fear and anxiety. So, discernment does not come with fear, but a knowing. Paranoia comes with fear and anxiety.

When people show you who you are, believe them. The Bible says that an evil tree cannot produce good fruit and a good tree cannot produce evil fruit (Matthew 7:18). Examine the fruit of every person's life with whom you interact.

CHAPTER 2

Why Are You Grieved In Any Relationship For A Friendship Of Any Kind?

*E*CCLESIASTES 1:14-18 READS, "14 *I have seen all the works that are done under the sun; and, behold, all is vanity and vexation of spirit.15 That which is crooked cannot be made straight: and that which is wanting cannot be numbered.16 I communed with mine own heart, saying, Lo, I am come to great estate, and have gotten more wisdom than all they that have been before me in Jerusalem: yea, my heart had great experience of wisdom and knowledge.17 And I gave my heart to know wisdom, and to know madness and folly: I perceived that this also is vexation of spirit.18 For in much wisdom is much grief: and he that increased knowledge increased sorrow."*

Matthew 26:36-39 reads, "36 Then Jesus came with them to a place called Gethsemane (olive-press), and He told His disciples, "Sit here while I go over there and pray." 37 And taking with Him Peter and the two sons of Zebedee [James and John], He began to be grieved and greatly distressed. 38 Then He said to them, "My soul is deeply grieved, so that I am almost dying of sorrow. Stay here and stay awake and keep watch with Me."39 And after going a little farther, He fell face down and prayed, saying, "My Father, if it is possible [that is, consistent with Your will], let this cup pass from Me; yet not as I will, but as You will."

Acts 16:16-18 reads, "And it came to pass, as we went to prayer, a certain damsel possessed with a spirit of divination met us, which brought her masters much gain by soothsaying:

17The same followed Paul and us, and cried, saying, these men are the servants of the highest God, which shew unto us the way of salvation.

18And this did she many days. But Paul, being grieved, turned, and said to the spirit, I command thee in the name of Jesus Christ to come out of her. And he came out the same hour."

You will be grieved when you are unequally yoked! Whether that is your boyfriend, fiancé, or husband. This is because your spirit man is sounding an alarm that something isn't okay or going on that you are unaware of but is a danger or threat to you! Don't ignore this warning. Take a step back. Spend some time alone with the Father and ask Him to show you what is grieving you.

When someone's motives and intentions are wrong, this will cause you to be grieved because your spirit man is discerning a potential danger if you go forward or proceed with the relationship, such as plans you have made with this person or any type of agreement you have made with someone in a business aspect or financial agreement. Don't make any sudden decisions at that time. Allow yourself some time to really examine which way the relationship, plans, or business and financial agreement is going or what the outcome will be. You never want to sign up for something that is easy to get into, but hard to get out of and cause you collateral damage.

You will be grieved when the following occurs:
- When you feel like you shouldn't do something
- When others are encouraging you to go forward with the idea of what you have when you don't really want it.
- When you are skeptical about it
- When you feel like you're going to be the one doing all the work, dedicating the most time, and spending the most resources.

There shouldn't be any compromise of your expectations concerning any friendship or relationship.

When you get that gut feeling, as a believer, it is the Holy Spirit warning you. Never override that feeling. God gave us emotions and feelings for a reason. It is for our natural defense and affects our decision-making. However, God did not give us the spirit of fear but of power, love, and a sound mind. I am not speaking of a feeling of anxiety. Anxiety comes from trauma. I'm talking about being in a situation that does not pose a physical threat to you now. This feeling is usually accurate and if you follow the warning by backing out of the agreement or not going forward in the relationship, you find peace. Be still and quiet. Time will reveal the reason you received the warning. The Holy Spirit will also give you an unction and you will just know what to do! I have said many times, "I don't know how I knew to do that," but I did. I was wrong. I knew what to do because of the Holy Spirit and yielding myself to Him.

1 John 2:20 says, *"But ye have an unction from the Holy One, and ye know all things. I have not written to you because you do not know the truth, but because you do know it, and because no lie is of the truth."* The Bible also says in *Luke 8:17, "For there is nothing hidden that will not become evident, nor anything secret that will not be known and come out into the open."* When we stand on Proverbs 3:5-6, we are not trusting in our own intellect or knowledge. We are depending on the Lord to give us directions.

There was an instance where I was in a relationship with a guy and at first, it was a head over heels experience. After the flames died down, I felt like I needed to leave this person. This would happen every time we argued or had any issues in our relationship. I knew in my heart that I deserved better than this person, even on a good day in our relationship. Little did I know was that this person was stealing from me, dragging my name through the mud to other women during their pillow talks, unfaithful, and never forgiving anyone for a mistake they made or if they did something to him that hurt his feelings or reputation. He had to have revenge. Moreover, he had an evil heart and would wish death upon people. It took me a while to get out of this relationship but I was grieved during the entire relationship. Once I got out of that relationship and moved into my own home, is when I had so much peace. It was peaceful being without him because I was unequally yoked and with someone who meant me no good.

Pay attention to your spirit when you are around people. Don't ever discredit what you're feeling. The Lord equipped us to know when something is not for us and could cause us harm.

CHAPTER 3

You Will Always Benefit From Persecution

*B*LESSED ARE THOSE WHO *are persecuted for righteousness' sake, for theirs is the kingdom of heaven. Blessed is those who are persecuted for righteousness' sake, for theirs is the kingdom of heaven. Blessed are you when others revile you and persecute you and utter all kinds of evil against you falsely on my account. Rejoice and be glad, for your reward is great in heaven, for so they persecuted the prophets who were before you (Matthew 5:10-12).*

Beloved, think it not strange concerning the fiery trial, which is to try you, as though some strange thing happened unto you: But rejoice, since ye are partakers of Christ's sufferings; that, when his glory shall be revealed, ye may be glad also with exceeding joy. If ye be reproached for the name of Christ, happy are ye; for the spirit of glory and of God rested upon you: on their part he is evil spoken of, but on your part, he is glorified (1 Peter 4:12-14).

James, a servant of God and of the Lord Jesus Christ, to the twelve tribes which are scattered abroad, greeting. My brethren, count it all joy when ye fall into divers temptations, knowing this, that the trying of your faith worketh patience. But let patience have her perfect work, that ye may be perfect and entire, wanting nothing (James 1:1-4).

In the Bible, everyone who suffered persecution suffered because of the name of Jesus Christ and the Word of God! Why would you suffer from being a believer and believing on the name of Jesus Christ as your Lord and Savior? Simply because it is the way to the kingdom of heaven. The enemy would love to keep you in a place of believing that your works will make you saved, or a good person, when that is the total opposite of God's Word. Jesus promised us in *Revelation 2:18-26,* "*And unto the angel of the church in Thyatira write; These things saith the Son of God, who hath his eyes like unto a flame of fire, and his feet are like fine brass; I know thy works, and charity, and service, and faith, and thy patience, and thy works; and the last to be more than the first. Notwithstanding I have a few things against thee, because thou suffer that woman Jezebel, which calleth herself a prophetess, to teach and to seduce my servants to commit fornication, and to eat things sacrificed unto idols. And I gave her space to repent of her fornication; and she repented not. Behold, I will cast her into a bed, and them that commit adultery with her into great tribulation, except they repent of their deeds. And I will kill her children with death; and all the churches shall know that I am her which searched the reins and hearts: and I will give unto every one of you according to your works. But unto you I say, and unto the rest in Thyatira, as many as have not this doctrine, and which*

13

have not known the depths of Satan, as they speak; I will put upon you none other burden. But that which ye have already hold fast till I come. And he that overcomes, and kept my works unto the end, to him will I give power over the nations."

Believers always benefit from persecution. *Revelation 12:9-11 reads, "And the great dragon was cast out, that old serpent, called the Devil, and Satan, which deceived the whole world: he was cast out into the earth, and his angels were cast out with him. And I heard a loud voice saying in heaven, Now is come salvation, and strength, and the kingdom of our God, and the power of his Christ: for the accuser of our brethren is cast down, which accused them before our God Day and night. And they overcame him by the blood of the Lamb, and by the word of their testimony; and they loved not their lives unto the death."*

Overcoming the persecution and temptation by the blood of the Lamb and the word of our testimony is very powerful. Neither one is something that we created or can do on our own. This means that "the Lord" is the one who helps us to overcome. The enemy can fight us as people in our flesh and always win. He can never win when he faces God.

Jesus Christ benefited from His persecution. The Apostle Paul explains in Hebrews Chapter one how Jesus benefited from being crucified, died, buried, resurrected, ascended into heaven, and is seated at the right hand of God, forever making intercession. *Hebrews 1:1-14 reads, "God, who at sundry times and in divers manners spoke in time past unto the fathers by the prophets, Hath in these last days spoken unto us by his Son, whom he hath appointed heir of all things, by whom also he made the worlds; Who being the brightness of his glory, and the express image of his person, and upholding all things by the word of his power, when he had by himself purged our sins, sat down on the right hand of the Majesty on high: Being made so much better than the angels, as he hath by inheritance obtained a more excellent name than they. For unto which of the angels said he at any time, thou art my son, this day have I begotten thee? And again, I will be to him a father, and he shall be to me a son? And again, when he bringeth in the first begotten into the world, he saith, and let all the angels of God worship him. And of the angels he saith, who makes his angels spirits, and his ministers a flame of fire. But unto the Son he saith, thy throne, O God, is for ever and ever: a scepter of righteousness is the scepter of thy kingdom. Thou hast loved righteousness, and hated iniquity; therefore God, even thy God, hath anointed thee with the oil of gladness above thy fellows. And Thou, Lord, in the beginning hast laid the foundation of the earth; and the heavens are the works of thine hands: They shall perish; but thou remain; and they all shall wax old as doth a garment; And as a vesture shalt thou fold them up, and they shall be changed: but thou art the same, and thy years shall not fail. But to which of the angels said he at any time, sit on my right hand, until I make thine enemies thy footstool? Are they not all ministering spirits, sent forth to minister for them who shall be heirs of salvation?"*

Noah was persecuted and benefited.

Genesis 6:8 says, "But Noah found grace in the eyes of the Lord." The people didn't listen to Noah. They mocked him because there was no rain. They couldn't picture or believe that a flood was coming, but Noah trusted God and it came to pass. "

Genesis 6:13-21 says, "And God said unto Noah, The end of all flesh is come before me; for the earth is filled with violence through them; and, behold, I will destroy them with the earth. Make thee an ark of gopher wood; rooms shalt thou make in the ark, and shalt pitch it within and without with pitch. And this is the fashion which thou shalt make it of: The length of the ark shall be three hundred cubits, the breadth of it fifty cubits, and the height of it thirty cubits. A window shalt thou make to the ark, and in a cubit shalt thou finish it above; and the door of the ark shalt thou set in the side thereof; with lower, second, and third stories shalt thou make it. And, behold, I, even I, do bring a flood of waters upon the earth, to destroy all flesh, wherein is the breath of life, from under heaven; and every thing that is in the earth shall die. But with thee will I establish my covenant; and thou shalt come into the ark, thou, and thy sons, and thy wife, and thy sons' wives with thee. And of every living thing of all flesh, two of every sort shalt thou bring into the ark, to keep them alive with thee; they shall be male and female. Of fowls after their kind, and of cattle after their kind, of every creeping thing of the earth after his kind, two of every sort shall come unto thee, to keep them alive. And take thou unto thee of all food that is eaten, and thou shalt gather it to thee; and it shall be for food for thee, and for them."

Genesis 7:9 says, "And the LORD said unto Noah, Come thou and all thy house into the ark; for thee have I seen righteous before me in this generation."

Joseph was persecuted and benefited.

Genesis 37:23-28 says, "And it came to pass, when Joseph was come unto his brethren, that they stripped Joseph out of his coat, his coat of many colors that was on him; And they took him and cast him into a pit: and the pit was empty, there was no water in it. And they sat down to eat bread: and they lifted their eyes and looked, and behold, a company of Ishmaelite's came from Gilead with their camels bearing spicery and balm and myrrh, going to carry it down to Egypt. And Judah said unto his brethren, what profit is it if we slay our brother, and conceal his blood? Come, and let us sell him to the Ishmaelite's, and let not our hand be upon him; for he is our brother and our flesh. And his brethren were content. Then there passed by Midianite's merchantmen; and they drew and lifted Joseph out of the pit and sold Joseph to the Ishmaelite's for twenty pieces of silver: and they brought Joseph into Egypt."

Genesis 41:39-43 says, "And Pharaoh said unto Joseph, Forasmuch as God hath shewed thee all this, there is none so discreet and wise as thou art: Thou shalt be over my house, and according unto thy word shall all my people be ruled: only in the throne will I be greater than thou. And Pharaoh said unto Joseph, See, I have set thee over all the land of Egypt. And Pharaoh took off his ring from his hand, and put it upon Joseph's hand, and arrayed him in vestures of fine linen, and put a gold chain about his neck; And he made him to ride in the second chariot which he had; and they cried before him, Bow the knee: and he made him ruler over all the land of Egypt."

WISDOM KEYS:

Never despise being persecuted because you will always benefit from the persecution if you don't fall away.

Blessed are those who are persecuted for righteousness' sake, for theirs is the kingdom of heaven. Blessed are you when others revile you and persecute you and utter all kinds of evil against you falsely on my account. Rejoice and be glad, for your reward is great in heaven, for so they persecuted the prophets who were before you (Matthew 5:10-12).

And ye now therefore have sorrow: but I will see you again, and your heart shall rejoice, and your joy no man taketh from you (John 16:22).

CHAPTER 4

Clean Hands and Pure Heart

W HY DO WE NEED a clean heart? The Bible points out numerous times that the Lord searches the reins of our hearts to see what is in us. This is found in *Jeremiah 17:10 which reads, "I the LORD search the heart, I try the reins, even to give every man according to his ways, and according to the fruit of his doings." Also, in Proverbs 20:27 the Lord says that the spirit of a man is the candle to the Lord which also refers to the inner most heart of man.*

This is explained by Ellicott's Commentary for English Readers in the Bible Hub. John Ellicott was a distinguished Christian theologian, academic, and church man. Ellicott's Commentary says in Proverbs 20:27, The spirit of man is the candle of the Lord. The spirit of man, breathed into him at first by the Creator (Genesis 2:7), and afterwards quickened and illumined by the Divine Spirit, is the "candle of the Lord," given to man as an inward light and guide. Searching all the inward parts of the belly. That is, of the inmost heart of man; testing all his thoughts, feelings, desires, by God's law, approving some, condemning others, according as they agree with it or not. The word "belly" is equivalent to "heart" or "soul" in Job 15:2; Job 15:15; Job 32:19, John 7:38.

We must have clean hands and a pure heart in order to ascend into the hill of the Lord. *Psalms 24:3-6 says, "Who shall ascend into the hill of the LORD? or who shall stand in his holy place? 4He that hath clean hands, and a pure heart, who hath not lifted up his soul unto vanity, nor sworn deceitfully. 5He shall receive the blessing from the LORD, and righteousness from the God of his salvation. 6This is the generation of them that seek him, that seek thy face, O Jacob. Selah."*

What is the hill of the Lord? According to the Blue Letter Bible, in the Strong's Concordance, H2022 "Har" is pronounced like "Hair." This is described as a: mountain, mount, hill, country, or promotion. The biblical usage is Hill, mountain, hill country, or mount. It is also a masculine noun, and we know that masculine nouns is a word for a man or a boy or male animals. In this context, the hill of the Lord is referring to "God Himself." God is a He. In numerous scriptures, the Lord describes himself as "I Am HE." This can be found in *Isaiah 43:1,13, and 25. Verse 1 reads, But now thus saith the LORD that created thee, O Jacob, and he that formed thee, O Israel, Fear not: for I have redeemed thee, I have called thee by thy name; thou art mine." Verse 13 reads, "Yea, before the day was I am he; and there is none that can deliver out of my hand: I will work, and who shall let it?" Verse 25 reads, "I, even I, am he that blotted out thy transgressions for mine own sake, and will not remember thy sins."*

Learning the meaning of where the Lord is saying we can ascend to is important. We know that a Hill is a High Place. As I picture this, it reminds me of Moses, when he would go up into the mountain to meet with God and receive instructions from the Lord. You can find this in *Exodus 19:3, which reads, "Then Moses went up to God, and the LORD called to him from the mountain and said, "This is what you are to say to the descendants of Jacob and what you are to tell the people of Israel."*

Abraham would offer sacrifices to God in the High Places. He even went up to Mount Moriah when he obeyed God concerning sacrificing Isaac. This can be found in *Genesis 22:2. It reads, "Take now your son, your only son Isaac, whom you love, and go to the LAND of MORIAH, and offer him ('lift him up') THERE for a burnt offering on one of the mountains which I will tell you of."*

Elijah was instructed by the Lord to come up on the mountain to meet Him on Mount Horeb. This is where the Lord allowed Elijah to see Him physically as He passed by and Elijah also received the revelation that the Lord was not in all the things that were loud or boisterous, things that cause fear and anxiety, but He is in the still small voice. 1 *Kings 19:11-13 reads, "He said, "Go out and stand on the mountain before the LORD, for the LORD is about to pass by." Now there was a great wind, so strong that it was splitting mountains and breaking rocks in pieces before the LORD, but the LORD was not in the wind; and after the wind an earthquake, but the LORD was not in the earthquake; and after the earthquake a fire, but the LORD was not in the fire; and after the fire a sound of sheer silence. When Elijah heard it, he wrapped his face in his mantle and went out and stood at the entrance of the cave. Then there came a voice to him that said, "What are you doing here, Elijah?"*

Even Jesus Christ "The Messiah," the Lord of Lords and the King of Kings went up into the mountain (the high place) to pray and be alone, after He would have taught His disciples and the multitudes of people. Jesus would sometimes take the disciples that He chose up in the mountain to teach them things that they needed to know about Him and so that they would believe that He was the Messiah. He also was transfigured and affirmed by God the Father in front of 3 witnesses: Peter, James, and John. He was not to be revealed until after He was raised from the dead. This is found in *Matthew 17:1-9, which reads, "and after six days Jesus taketh Peter, James, and John his brother, and bringeth them up into a high mountain apart, and was transfigured before them: and his face did shine as the sun, and his raiment was white as the light. And behold, there appeared unto them Moses and Elias talking with him. Then answered Peter, and said unto Jesus, Lord, it is good for us to be here: if thou wilt, let us make here three tabernacles; one for thee, and one for Moses, and one for Elias. While he yet spoke, behold, a bright cloud overshadowed them: and behold a voice out of the cloud, which said, this is my beloved Son, in whom I am well pleased; hear ye him. And when the disciples heard it, they fell on their face, and were sore afraid. And Jesus came and touched them, and said, Arise, and be not afraid. And when they had lifted their eyes, they saw no man, save Jesus only. And as they came down from the mountain, Jesus charged them, saying, Tell the vision to no man, until the Son of man be risen again from the dead."*

Let's talk about the transfiguration of Jesus Christ. Transfigured is defined in the Oxford Dictionary (2022) as "transform into something more beautiful or elevated."

A. In the Blue Letter Bible /Strong's Concordance: is the Greek word G3339 metamorphoo and is pronounced as metam-or-fo-o and is a verb and defined as: transfigure or transform or change. The biblical usage in this scripture is interpreted as "to change into another form, to transform, to transfigure. Christ's appearance was changed and was resplendent with divine brightness on the mount of transfiguration.

B. Christ's appearance was changed and was resplendent with divine brightness on the mount of transfiguration.

Now that we know why we need Clean Hands & A Pure Heart, which is to be able to go into the high place where God dwells. The various people that I outlined tonight went into the High place for either the same or different reasons. We know from the scriptures when you are able to ascend into the hill of the Lord:

1. Receive clarity, instructions, directions, understanding, and wisdom from God.
2. Offer sacrifices of worship to God for the things He has done.
3. Offer sacrifices He requires from you.
4. Pray and become closer to God
5. Receive your affirmation.

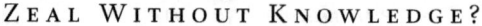

6. Learn who God is.

7. Be transformed or changed by God.

CHAPTER 5

The Importance Of Submission To God And Following the Leading Of The Holy Spirit

MATTHEW 4:1-11 READS, " *Then Jesus was led by the Spirit into the wilderness to be tempted by the devil. After fasting forty days and forty nights, he was hungry. 3The tempter came to him and said, "If you are the Son of God, tell these stones to become bread." Jesus answered, "It is written: 'Man shall not live on bread alone, but on every word that comes from the mouth of God.'" Then the devil took him to the holy city and had him stand on the highest point of the temple. 6 "If you are the Son of God," he said, "throw yourself down. For it is written "'He will command his angels concerning you, and they will lift you up in their hands, so that you will not strike your foot against a stone.' Jesus answered him, "It is also written: 'Do not put the Lord your God to the test.'" Again, the devil took him to a very high mountain and showed him all the kingdoms of the world and their splendor. "All this I will give you," he said, "if you will bow down and worship me." Jesus said to him, "Away from me, Satan! For it is written: 'Worship the Lord your God, and serve him only.' " Then the devil left him, and angels came and attended him."*

Considering the scriptures, you must be submitted to God to overcome every temptation and to be led by the Holy Spirit. Jesus fasted for forty days and forty nights and was able to overcome all the temptation that would come His way during the time of His ministry. Jesus received power over His flesh (His carnal nature) and was led by the Holy Spirit, which also means He was "able to walk in the Spirit." Romans 8:14 *reads, "for as many as are led by the Spirit of God, they are the Sons of God."* Jesus confirmed His identity as a Son of God 3 times. Also, submission increases your discernment. When you are submitted to God and led by the Holy Spirit, you will be a steward of the Word of God. The Word of God says that *strong meat belongs to them that can discern good from evil (Hebrews 5:14).* Because Jesus was the living Word. He was also able to discern when the enemy tried to use the Word of God incorrectly to deceive him. This means that the enemy will try to use the Word of God against us to tempt us if we do not know the Word of God and have discernment of the enemy's tactics. We know here that Jesus Christ is the Living Word and was the Word in the Flesh while He was on the earth. His discernment was keen and on point. If we want to discern good from evil, we must eat the meat of God's Word.

During Jesus's temptation, His identity was questioned in all three attempts. The enemy had to see if Jesus really knew who He was and how He would respond when someone questioned His identity. Jesus proved to the devil that His submission to God the Father and was authentic and He was obedient to the Holy Spirit and allowed Him to lead him. This is a work that God did in Jesus through His submission and following the Holy Spirit, which was genuine and everlasting. You will only be solid in your identity when you are submitted to God. Submission leads to surrender. Surrender means "submitting your authority to someone and is an action of yielding." If you can submit to God and follow the Holy Spirit that means you trust God. *Jeremiah 17:5-6 says, "Blessed is the man that trusts in God and cursed is the man who puts his trust in man." Thus says the LORD, "Cursed is the man who trusts in and relies on mankind, making [weak, faulty human] flesh his strength, and whose mind and heart turn away from the LORD." Psalms 40:4 says, "lesser [fortunate, prosperous, and favored by God] is the man who makes the LORD his trust and does not regard the proud nor those who lapse into lies."*

In the first temptation of the devil, Jesus overcame the temptation of hunger. The enemy knew that Jesus had been fasting and tried to lead Jesus back into the fleshly realm to remove His submission to God. The enemy tried to get Jesus to use the power that God gave Him incorrectly for a fleshly desire.

When the enemy said to Him, "If You Are the Son of God, tell these stones to become bread." He was tempting Jesus to give up His birth right as the Son of God. Jesus was the "Son of God" already, God's only begotten Son. His identity was revealed to Mary and Joseph upon His conception in *Matthew*

1:18-25 which reads, "Now the birth of Jesus Christ was on this wise: When as his mother Mary was espoused to Joseph, before they came together, she was found with child of the Holy Ghost. Then Joseph her husband, being a just man, and not willing to make her a public example, was minded to put her away privily. But while he thought on these things, behold, the angel of the LORD appeared unto him in a dream, saying, Joseph, thou son of David, fear not to take unto thee Mary thy wife: for that which is conceived in her is of the Holy Ghost. And she shall bring forth a son, and thou shalt call his name JESUS: for he shall save his people from their sins. Now all this was done, that it might be fulfilled which was spoken of the Lord by the prophet, saying, Behold, a virgin shall be with child, and shall bring forth a son, and they shall call his name Emmanuel, which being interpreted is, God with us. Then Joseph being raised from sleep did as the angel of the Lord had bidden him, and took unto him his wife: And knew her not till she had brought forth her firstborn son: and he called his name JESUS."

Esau was in a similar situation as Jesus Christ with the temptation of hunger and bread but Jesus didn't give in to the temptation or the hunger.

Genesis 25:29-34 reads, "Once when Jacob was cooking stew, Esau came in from the field, and he was exhausted. And Esau said to Jacob, "Let me eat some of that red stew, for I am exhausted!" (Therefore his name was called Edom.) Jacob said, "Sell me your birthright now." Esau said, "I am about to die; of what use is a birthright to me?" Jacob said, "Swear to me now." So he swore to him and sold his birthright to Jacob. Then Jacob gave Esau bread and lentil stew, and he ate and drank and rose and went his way. Thus, Esau despised his birthright."

In the end, Esau sold his birth right for bread, lentil stew, and something to drink. After his hunger was fulfilled, he despised his decision, but it was too late for him. This was not a lasting reward. It was temporal. The Bible says the things that are seen are temporal, but the things that are not seen are eternal. This is found in *2 Corinthians 4:18 which reads, "While we look not at the things which are seen, but at the things which are not seen: for the things which are seen are temporal; but the things which are not seen are eternal. Never give up your eternal blessing for earthly possessions."*

This temptation also was a question of Jesus's identity. Jesus's identity was already established when Mary conceived Him by the Holy Spirit and the Lord visited Joseph to help him understand "The Virgin Birth" of Jesus Christ. The angel of the Lord instructed Joseph and Mary on what Jesus's name should be while He was an unborn child. The Angel of the Lord revealed the meaning of His name to Joseph: "He will save His people from His sins" and means that He is their savior.

Jesus was already promised to the children of Israel (the Jews) as the "Messiah." The Oxford Dictionary defines "Messiah" as the promised deliverer of the Jewish nation prophesied in the Hebrew Bible." The identity of Jesus had already been revealed in the Old Testament to Isaiah the prophet and established in *Matthew 1:18-25, which reads, "Now the birth of Jesus Christ was on this wise: When as his mother Mary was espoused to Joseph, before they came together, she was found with child of the Holy Ghost. Then Joseph her husband, being a just man, and* not willing to make her a public example, was minded to put her away privily. But while he thought on these things, behold, the angel of the LORD appeared unto him in a dream, saying, Joseph, thou son of David, fear not to take unto thee Mary thy wife: for that which is conceived in her is of the Holy Ghost. And she shall bring forth a son, and thou shalt call his name JESUS: for he shall save his people from their sins. Now all this was done, that it might be fulfilled which was spoken of the Lord by the prophet, saying, Behold, a virgin shall be with child, and shall bring forth a son, and they shall call his name Emmanuel, which being interpreted is, God with us. Then Joseph being raised from sleep did as the angel of the Lord had bidden him and took unto him his wife: And knew her not till she had brought forth her firstborn son: and he called his name JESUS." Not only was Jesus's identity revealed before His birth, but He also was conceived of the Holy Spirit. Jesus's name was established as "Emmanuel" which means "God is with us," prior to his conception or birth. This can be found in Isaiah 7:14, which reads, "Therefore, the Lord himself shall give you a sign; Behold, a virgin shall conceive, and bear a son, and shall call his name Immanuel."

Anytime the enemy comes against your identity, it is to cause you not to walk in your "God-given identity," which is the opposite of being submitted to God. You will do things your own way because you don't understand that God is the one that gives you an assignment. Jesus Christ was given an assignment by God, and He knew His assignment. His submission helped Him to fulfill the purpose, call, and destiny given to Him by God the Father before He was conceived. This is reflected in the Old Testament in many instances.

The enemy tempted Jesus Christ to see if He had any weaknesses or carnal desires that would cause Him to disobey God. The devil wanted Jesus to give over to him what God had already given to Jesus. This was also an assassination attempt in a subtle way. The devil knew he could not take away Jesus's power and that Jesus had power over him, so he offered Jesus something of this world, earthly possessions to bribe Him and steal His eternal promise given to Him by God the Father.

God the Father promised Jesus that He would sit at the right hand of God and have all power and authority. This is found in several scriptures, with Jesus affirming what the Father had already revealed to Him. Jesus walked in the wisdom of God and opposed every threat to His assignment.

Here are a few scriptures where Jesus prophesied or revealed to His disciples, the Pharisees, and the Sadducees about who he was:

Matthew 26:64 says, "Jesus said to him, "You have said so. But I tell you, from now on you will see the Son of Man seated at the right hand of Power and coming on the clouds of heaven."

Matthew 22:44 says, "The Lord said to my Lord, sit at my right hand, until I put your enemies under your feet."

Matthew 28:18 says, "And Jesus came and said to them, "All authority in heaven and on earth has been given to me."

Matthew 25:31 says, "When the Son of Man comes in his glory, and all the angels with him, then he will sit on his glorious throne."

Matthew 20:21 says, "And he said to her, "What do you want?"
She said to him, "Say that these two sons of mine are to sit, one at
your right hand and one at your left, in your kingdom."

Jesus was so submitted to God and the Holy Spirit that He
was solid in his purpose. Nothing could stop Him from fulfill-
ing the purpose and destiny of God through His submission
and surrender.

The main reason we need to submit to God and follow the
leading of the Holy Spirit ultimately is to gain the eternal promise of eternal life that is given to us in *John 3:16, which reads,*
"For God so loved the world, that he gave his only begotten Son,
that whosoever believeth in him should not perish, but have ever-
lasting life."

The Bible also tells us that the "Holy Spirit" is a down payment of the promise that God the Father has given to those who
have received His Son Jesus Christ as their Lord and Savior and
believe in their hearts that He raised Him from the dead. This
is found in *Ephesians 1:13-14. The CEB (Common English Bi-*
ble) translation reads, "You too heard the word of truth in Christ,
which is the good news of your salvation. You were sealed with
the promised Holy Spirit because you believed in Christ. The Holy
Spirit is the down payment on our inheritance, which is applied
toward our redemption as God's own people, resulting in the honor
of God's glory." The King James Version reads, *"In whom ye also*
trusted, after that ye heard the word of truth, the gospel of your
salvation: in whom also after that ye believed, ye were sealed with
that holy Spirit of promise, which is the earnest of our inheritance

until the redemption of the purchased possession, unto the praise of his glory."

THE RESULT OF SUBMISSION AND BEING LED BY THE SPIRIT OF GOD.

Matthew 22:14 reads, "For many are called, but few are chosen." Jesus spoke this after He gave the parable of what the kingdom of heaven is like when someone is invited to the wedding of Jesus Christ. In this parable, the King invited people initially to come into his home, but they didn't show up. So, he sent his servants to go into the street to call strangers into the wedding and gave them garments, and they came to the wedding. One of the strangers that was called came into the wedding without putting on his garments and the servant was bound hand and foot and cast into outer darkness, where there is weeping and gnashing of teeth.

The man who was called to the wedding did not submit to the rules of his invitation. He didn't put on the garments given to him and was appropriate to attend the wedding. This signifies that he was not submitted to the rulership of the King, but he still wanted to attend the wedding and receive the benefits of being invited to the wedding. The King required the garments he provided as the only requisition to enter the wedding. The man was not submitted to the person who invited him to the wedding and was cast into outer darkness (hell).

The reason many are called but few are chosen is because of their will. Submission to God and being led by the Holy Spirit are directly related to one's will. You can be told or called to do something, but you won't submit to the prerequisites to be chosen.

I see the "many are called" as those who are called by God from eternity, and the chosen are those who are called and selected to enter the kingdom of God and receive the benefits of His Son Jesus Christ because they were submitted to the Word of God and followed the leading of the Holy Spirit.

Many people love the sound of going to heaven, being blessed, receiving eternal life, being called kings and priests on the earth, work in signs, wonders and miracles, preach and teach the gospel. Still, they have not fulfilled the prerequisites to obtain the benefits of the Kingdom of Heaven.

I have a few scriptures that will be good for your study time in helping you to determine if you are "called" and "chosen" or if you are just "called" and have not been chosen.

The scriptures are:

Matthew 7:21: Not everyone who says to Me, 'Lord, Lord,' will enter the kingdom of heaven, but only he who does the will of My Father who is in heaven.

Matthew 7:13-1: Enter ye in at the strait gate: for wide is the gate, and broad is the way, that leadeth to destruction, and many there be which go in there at: Because strait is the gate, and narrow is the way, which leadeth unto life, and few there be that find it.

James 4:7: Submit yourselves therefore to God. Resist the devil, and he will flee from you.

Matthew 16:2: Then said Jesus unto his disciples, if any man will come after me, let him deny himself, and take up his cross, and follow me.

I pray it opened your eyes and pierced your heart to examine yourself to see if you are a "Chosen One" or just a "Called One."

CHAPTER 6

Double-Mindedness Is Your Enemy

*T*HE BIBLE GIVES MANY instances of people or leaders who were double minded in their faith or walk with God.

In the Blue Letter Bible-Strong's Concordance, double-minded is defined in James 1-8 as wavering, uncertain, doubting, or divided in interest. This is a Greek word in the Bible and the reference in the Strong's Concordance is G1374. This is an adjective. An adjective is defined as a word or phrase naming an attribute, added to, or grammatically related to a noun to modify or describe it. Here the word "double-minded" is describing the attribute of a man i.e., person, which is the noun. The word double-minded is the Greek word "Dipsychos" or "dip-soo-khos." Strong's definitions legend also has two other Greek references for double-minded. G1364 and G5590 means two spirited, i.e., or vacilating (in opinion or purpose).

James 1:5-8 reads, "Now if any of you lacks wisdom, he should ask God, who gives generously to all without finding fault, and it will be given to him. 6But he must ask in faith, without doubting, because he who doubts is like a wave of the sea, blown and tossed by the wind. 7That man should not expect to receive anything from the Lord. 8He is a double-minded man, unstable in all his ways."

The Bible is adamant about having faith in God and that anything outside of faith is a sin. All the promises that God has made to those who believe in His Only Begotten Son Jesus Christ, and that He raised Him from the dead are listed in the Bible.

How does that look in a believer's life? I believe that it should be the same for every believer. However, it is based upon their faith and how close they walk with God. I believe this determines the promises that a believer will receive from God.

For example, I may have faith that is strong in knowing that God is my healer because I have experienced His healing before. I have faith that no disease or affliction can dwell in my body, and there is nothing that anyone can tell me that can change my mind. This type of faith is what gets the attention of God! Because of my faith in Him and knowing the promise to me for healing in my body in the Bible and speaking that over myself will manifest for me because I believed. If I would stand on *Isaiah 53:5 which says, "Jesus was wounded for my transgressions and bruised for my iniquities and the chastisement of his peace is upon me and by his stripes I am healed and whole."*

However, another person may not be strong in their faith for healing, but they are strong in believing God for provision, their needs, and finances. This may be because they have experienced hard times before and know that God has delivered them from the worst situations that you could face in life, such as eviction, hunger, being jobless, unable to pay their electricity bill, not having food and so on. If their faith is unwavering in this area, they won't be shaken when any situation arises in their lives that would cause them to be oppressed by the spirit of poverty. They may be standing on *Psalms 112:5 which reads, "Wealth and riches are in my house, but my righteousness endures forever."*

This is called unwavering faith or being single minded, one-minded or for sure. This is having hope and faith mixed, while allowing your hope in God to be the foundation of your faith. In both instances, they are promised in the Bible. I am promised healing and wealth according to the Word of God.

Isaiah 55:9-11 reads, "For as the heavens are higher than the earth, so are my ways higher than your ways, and my thoughts than your thoughts. For as the rain cometh down, and the snow from heaven, and returned not thither, but watered the earth, and makes it bring forth and bud, that it may give seed to the Sower, and bread to the eater: So shall my word be that goeth forth out of my mouth: it shall not return unto me void, but it shall accomplish that which I please, and it shall prosper in the thing whereto I sent it."

Matthew 17:15-20 reads, "Lord, have mercy on my son: for he is lunatic, and sore vexed: for ofttimes he falleth into the fire, and oft into the water. And I brought him to thy disciples, and they

38

could not cure him. Then Jesus answered and said, O faithless and perverse generation, how long shall I be with you? how long shall I suffer you? bring him hither to me. And Jesus rebuked the devil; and he departed out of him: and the child was cured from that very hour. Then came the disciples to Jesus apart, and said, why could not we cast him out? And Jesus said unto them, Because of your unbelief: for verily I say unto you, if ye have faith as a grain of mustard seed, ye shall say unto this mountain, remove hence to yonder place; and it shall remove; and nothing shall be impossible unto you."

This scripture defines being single-minded, unwavering in our faith and being sure that God watches over His Word to ensure it is performed according to *Jeremiah 1:10-12. The Lord spoke to the prophet Jeremiah and said, "See, I have appointed you this day over the nations and over the kingdoms, to uproot and break down, to destroy and to overthrow, to build and to plant."*

THE ALMOND BRANCH AND BOILING POT:

The word of the LORD came to me, saying, "Jeremiah, what do you see?" And I said, "I see the branch of an [b]almond tree." 12 Then the LORD said to me, "You have seen well, for I am [actively] watching over My word to fulfill it."

Timothy teaches us in 2 Timothy 2:11-13 of a trust-worthy saying which means:

This is a trustworthy saying:
• 	If we die with Him, we will also live with Him.

- If we endure, we will also reign with Him.
- If we deny Him, He will also deny us.
- If we are faithless, He remains faithful, for He cannot deny Himself.

The Lord's honesty and truthfulness are being taught and revealed to us.

We must have unwavering faith to obtain the promises that God has given us in His Word. I believe that a double-minded person is leaning to their own understanding. When I say this, I mean that they are relying on their human abilities, trying to picture or figure out how whatever they believe God for what is going to happen, worrying about the beginning of something and how it will end.

Instead of believing the scripture in *Romans 8:28, which reads in the Amplified Bible, "And we know [with great confidence] that God [who is deeply concerned about us] causes all things to work together [as a plan] for good for those who love God, to those who are called according to His plan and purpose."*

The key word in this scripture is ALL Things. If we would meditate on the scriptures, I believe that we would have stronger faith. Especially if you believe in God and you are totally dependent on Him for everything you need.

I went through a season in the spring of 2021 that caused my faith to be increased. My realtor and I both worked in the same area at our place of employment. As we were working I explained to her that I was trying to purchase a home with a low-income home purchase program. She immediately told me that I didn't have to go that route. I didn't believe her, but she was persistent in trying to recruit me to purchase a home. I would even hide from her or go the other way sometimes because I was judging what I felt I was worthy of and could achieve. She had faith and trusted that God was in my life. I didn't feel like I deserved anything that God was doing for me, so I had wavering faith concerning purchasing a home. Although I was approved for home loans I was still discouraged when I was viewing homes with my realtor. After viewing the 10th home in Charlotte and trying to bid on the homes for earnest money that I would offer, every single time someone else would out bid me and the home would be gone as quickly as we had viewed it.

I became discouraged and wanted to quit. I told my realtor that I would like to stop and that I didn't want to pursue the purchasing process at that time. It was so stressful for me. I was discouraged and even questioned God concerning my vision board created for me and my family. I totally forgot that I had placed the purchase of a home on every single vision board each year starting in 2016. I had settled in my heart after I reviewed everything that I would be paying financially by purchasing a home. This included: mortgage, in certain cases, homeowner's association fees, taxes, trash, and water bill, etc.. I had gotten comfortable with the costs of living in an apartment and enjoyed having the extra money every month. I also saw obtaining a home as "scary." I was fearful of failing, being foreclosed or not being able to live a comfortable life as a home buyer.

My realtor never gave up. She never took no for an answer. When I refused to view anymore homes, she was still searching. She had faith and was sure that God had promised me the home I wanted. Maybe a month later, she called me and said to me, "I know you said you don't want to see any more homes, but I have found a home that you might really like." She knew my taste because I told her exactly what I was looking for and that I wouldn't budge on the bonus room because I liked to have a lot of space. She said, "If you can just come and view it." I agreed and met her one afternoon after work at the model home. When I walked in, I was flabbergasted. It was everything I desired and was so spacious, and guess what? It had a bonus room! There was plenty of yard space and my home wasn't even built yet.

During our viewing, the builder's representative began to explain the process. Guess what? This was the easiest process ever. I couldn't believe it because of the home buyers' trauma I faced in Charlotte (lol). She told me that there was a waiting list because the builder would start to build, order lumber and such when someone was under contract. Literally a week later, I was the first person on the list. I had to put down my earnest money. Guess what? God had just blessed me with a lump sum of money, and I was able to put down my money. The next week, I started receiving emails about the process of the stages the builder was in. This begins with choosing my lot and building the foundation. I was still in disbelief. I didn't think that the contract was serious. I thought, "This might be a scam because it is too easy." I was even able to select the area of land I wanted my home on, whether in the front, middle or back of the development and if I wanted it against the wood line.

I believe that God responded to my faith that I had in Him for the 5 years I believed and was unwavering, while also showing me grace as believing that God watches over His Word to ensure it was performed. I held on to the promise and was persistent in my request and was like Jacob when he wrestled with God. This can be found in Genesis 32:22-32. I am going to expound on this scripture in another teaching.

It is so amazing. The Lord has literally fulfilled everything I placed on my vision board for years. There is only one thing left, and that is a husband. I believe that he is coming.

I had a fear of "success," which was a sin. The Bible says anytime we don't have faith, we are sinning against God. *Romans 14:23 (NLT) reads, "23 But if you have doubts about whether or not you should eat something, you are sinning if you go ahead and do it. For you are not following your convictions. If you do anything you believe is not right, you are sinning."*

This is referencing our belief in our salvation through Christ Jesus and not being double-minded. The word "doubt" in this scripture is the Greek reference # in the Strong's Concordance: G1252. The Greek word here is Dee-ak-ree-no.

The KJV translates Strong's G1252 in the following manner: doubt (5x), judge (3x), discern (2x), contend (2x), waver (2x), miscellaneous (5x).

We never want to be on the opposite end of God concerning our faith. If we want to be on the receiving end, we must believe that with Him, all things are possible. No matter what it is, the opposition you may face, anyone who is contending against you for various reasons, and your desire to receive the promises written in God's Word.

Hebrews Chapter 11 is a great place to start if you want your faith to be increased. It is a great example of the people who were believers and how they received the promises of God. It was because of their faith, such as ABEL, ENOCH, ABRAHAM, ISAAC, JACOB, SARA, ESAU, JOSEPH, AND MOSES.

We must have faith in God no matter what! Hebrews 11:1 says that faith is the result of things we hope for, and the evidence of things that we do not see. Faith is not in our flesh, but it is in our spirit. We will talk more about building your faith and confidence in God in later teachings.

CHAPTER 7

Being a Fruitful Believer

Being fruitful is one of the first commandments that man kind received after we were created in the beginning. You can find many instances in the Bible where the Lord told His son or daughter about being fruitful. Let's go over some of the scriptures and dive into why being fruitful as a believer is important.

It all begins in Genesis 1:26-31 which reads:

26And God said, let us make man in our image, after our likeness: and let them have dominion over the fish of the sea, and over the fowl of the air, and over the cattle, and over all the earth, and over every creeping thing that creepeth upon the earth.

27So God created man in his own image, in the image of God created he him; male and female created he them.

28And God blessed them, and God said unto them, be fruitful, and multiply, and replenish the earth, and subdue it: and have dominion over the fish of the sea, and over the fowl of the air, and over every living thing that moved upon the earth.

29And God said, Behold, I have given you every herb bearing seed, which is upon the face of all the earth, and every tree, in the which is the fruit of a tree yielding seed; to you it shall be for meat.

30And to every beast of the earth, and to every fowl of the air, and to everything that creepeth upon the earth, wherein there is life, I have given every green herb for meat: and it was so.

31And God saw everything that he had made, and behold, it was very good. And the evening and the morning were the sixth day.

God saw man as being good and because He desired for humanity to be fruitful, He also gave us dominion over everything He created. Every animal, plant, tree, etc., God provided everything we needed to be fruitful from the beginning.

It is our choice to choose if we are going to be fruitful and multiply as a believer. Everything we need to be fruitful through Jesus Christ has already been given to us. How has it been given to us? 2 Peter 1:1-4 explains how we have been given everything we need. *"Simon Peter, a servant and an apostle of Jesus Christ, to them that have obtained like precious faith with us through the righteousness of God and our Savior Jesus Christ: Grace and peace be multiplied unto you through the knowledge of God, and of Jesus our Lord, According as his divine power hath given unto us all things that pertain unto life and godliness, through the knowledge of him that hath called us to glory and virtue: Whereby are given unto us exceeding great and precious promises: that by these ye might be partakers of the divine nature, having escaped the corruption that is in the world through lust."*

This is another way that you will walk in faith to receive what God has given us in the earth to be fruitful. This is not something that you have to think your way through. This is something that God the Father will give you and reveal to you through your intimacy with Him in prayer, consecration and reading His Word. To be fruitful, having a close relationship with God it is vital. You will need his direction, insight, and wisdom. How you spend your time during your walk with God will determine your fruitfulness. We see here that you can only be fruitful through the KNOWLEDGE of Jesus Christ. This means that we must know Him, who He is, what He has done, and what He is doing now. Jesus was the prime example of being fruitful as you read the Gospel of Jesus Christ, which is in Matthew, Mark, Luke, and John. Jesus's life exemplified fruitfulness. Jesus was fruitful even with knowing that He was being persecuted for righteousness's sake, overcoming the temptations of the enemy, being led by the spirit, spending time alone with God, and speaking the truth to those who were blinded by the prince of this world and those who were religious, without the fruit or spirit of God abiding with them. The source of us being fruitful is strongly connected to us studying and knowing the Word of God.

When you are fruitful, you have peace, even in the face of adversity. Being fruitful brings God delight and us in return. When we are fruitful, the blessing of God flows freely in our lives. Blessings can be healing in our bodies, restoration in our homes within our family relationships, salvation for our loved ones, deliverance, wholeness, prosperity, and dominion.

John 15:1-11 explains this to us clearly. The price that Jesus Christ, the Son of the living God, paid for our sins exceeds the wisdom that we hold here on earth. It is only revealed by the Spirit of God, which is the Holy Spirit. Studying the scripture will open your eyes and give you wisdom on how to be fruitful.

I am the true vine, and my father is the husbandman.

2Every branch in me that beareth not fruit he taketh away: and every branch that beareth fruit, he purged it, that it may bring forth more fruit.

3Now ye are clean through the word which I have spoken unto you.

4Abide in me, and I in you. As the branch cannot bear fruit of itself, except it abide in the vine; no more can ye, except ye abide in me.

5I am the vine, ye are the branches: He that abided in me, and I in him, the same bringeth forth much fruit: for without me ye can do nothing.

6If a man abides not in me, he is cast forth as a branch, and is withered; and men gather them, and cast them into the fire, and they are burned.

7If ye abide in me, and my words abide in you, ye shall ask what ye will, and it shall be done unto you.

8Herein is my Father glorified, that ye bear much fruit; so, shall ye be my disciples.

9As the father hath loved me, so have I loved you: continue ye in my love.

10If ye keep my commandments, ye shall abide in my love; even as I have kept my father's commandments and abide in his love.

11These things have I spoken unto you, that my joy might remain in you, and that your joy might be full.

As a believer, being fruitful is necessary to please the Father and have eternal life in heaven when you pass away.

When you are abiding in Jesus Christ, allow the Father, God to take care of you, prune you and receive everything you need pertaining to life and godliness through the knowledge of Jesus Christ. Without abiding in the Word of God, intimacy with God the Father, and being unfruitful is a believer's enemy. The enemy of our soul is carnality. When we abide in Jesus Christ, we will walk in the Spirit. The key to abiding in Jesus Christ so that your fruit will remain is by allowing the Holy Spirit to lead and guide you in your walk with God. This is clearly written in Romans 8:6-16 which reads:

6For to be carnally minded is death; but to be spiritually minded is life and peace.

7Because the carnal mind is enmity against God: for it is not subject to the law of God, neither indeed can be.

8So then they that are in the flesh cannot please God.

9But ye are not in the flesh, but in the Spirit, if so be that the Spirit of God dwell in you. Now if any man has not the Spirit of Christ, he is none of his.

10And if Christ be in you, the body is dead because of sin; but the Spirit is life because of righteousness.

11But if the Spirit of him that raised up Jesus from the dead dwell in you, he that raised up Christ from the dead shall also quicken your mortal bodies by his Spirit that dwelleth in you.

12Therefore, brethren, we are debtors, not to the flesh, to live after the flesh.

13For if ye live after the flesh, ye shall die: but if ye through the Spirit do mortify the deeds of the body, ye shall live.

14For as many as are led by the Spirit of God, they are the sons of God.

15For ye have not received the spirit of bondage again to fear; but ye have received the Spirit of adoption, whereby we cry, Abba, Father.

16The Spirit itself beareth witness with our spirit, that we are the children of God:

As we walk in the Spirit, God opens the seals of His Word, and provides us with revelation that is filled with the knowledge of Jesus Christ and what we have obtained through Him. Our job as believers is to receive the promise that was given to us from the beginning. This is found in *John 3:16, when we received salvation. "For God so [greatly] loved and dearly prized the world, that He [even] gave His [One and] only begotten Son, so that whoever believes and trusts in Him [as Savior] shall not perish but have eternal life."* Eternal life in heaven with God the Father and Jesus Christ means worshipping at His feet day and night and not being cast into the lake of fire for eternity with the devil and his demons. God reveals in *2 Timothy 2:20* that some believers or members of the Body of Christ are for honor and some for dishonor. Verse 20-21 reads, *"20 But in a great house there are not only vessels of gold and silver, but also of wood and clay, some for honor and some for dishonor. 21 Therefore if anyone cleanses himself from the latter, he will be a vessel for hon-*

or, [h]sanctified and useful for the Master, prepared for every good work.”

EXAMPLES OF BEING FRUITFUL

You will obtain spiritually and have the fruits of the Spirit active in your everyday life. They are listed in *Galatians 5:22-25: But the fruit of the Spirit is love, joy, peace, longsuffering, gentleness, goodness, faith, Meekness, temperance: against such there is no law. And they that are Christ's have crucified the flesh with the affections and lusts. If we live in the Spirit, let us also walk in the Spirit. Let us not be desirous of vain glory, provoking one another, envying one another.*

Fruitlessness is also explained in *Galatians 5:19-21* and is a result of walking in our flesh, i.e., allowing our fleshly mind, will and emotions to rule over our life.

19 Now the practices of the sinful nature are clearly evident: they are sexual immorality, impurity, sensuality (total irresponsibility, lack of self-control), 20 idolatry, sorcery, hostility, strife, jealousy, fits of anger, disputes, dissensions, factions [that promote heresies], 21 envy, drunkenness, riotous behavior, and other things like these. I warn you beforehand, just as I did previously, that those who practice such things will not inherit the kingdom of God.

Righteousness produces fruitfulness and sin produces death. This is what Jesus Christ is explaining to us in *John 15:4-6.*

51

4Abide in me, and I in you. As the branch cannot bear fruit of itself, except it abide in the vine; no more can ye, except ye abide in me.

I am the vine, ye are the branches: He that abided in me, and I in him, the same bringeth forth much fruit: for without me ye can do nothing.

6If a man abides not in me, he is cast forth as a branch, and is withered; and men gather them, and cast them into the fire, and they are burned.

Matthew 7:15-20 (AMP) reads:

15 "Beware of the false prophets, [teachers] who come to you dressed as sheep [appearing gentle and innocent], but inwardly are ravenous wolves. 16 By their fruit you will recognize them [that is, by their contrived doctrine and self-focus]. Do people pick grapes from thorn bushes or figs from thistles? 17 Even so, every healthy tree bears good fruit, but the unhealthy tree bears bad fruit. 18 A good tree cannot bear bad fruit, nor can a bad tree bear good fruit. 19 Every tree that does not bear good fruit is cut down and thrown into the fire. 20 Therefore, by their fruit you will recognize them [as false prophets].

Again, Jesus is explaining to His disciples about producing fruit and pointing out that those who bear bad fruit are cast into the fire. This is mentioned in John 15 as well. We know that the fire is Hell. The abyss is the lake of fire.

Lastly, *2 Peter 1:3-11* explains to us the process of developing fruit in Jesus Christ and how they are connected to one another, which reads:

3 For His divine power has bestowed on us [absolutely] everything necessary for [a dynamic spiritual] life and godliness, through [d]true and personal knowledge of Him who called us by His own glory and excellence. 4 For by these He has bestowed on us His precious and magnificent promises [of inexpressible value], so that by them you may escape from the immoral freedom that is in the world because of disreputable desire and become sharers of the divine nature. 5 For this very reason, applying your diligence [to the divine promises, make every effort] in [exercising] your faith to, [e]develop moral excellence, and in moral excellence, knowledge (insight, understanding), 6 and in your knowledge, self-control, and in your self-control, steadfastness, and in your steadfastness, godliness, 7 and in your godliness, brotherly affection, and in your brotherly affection, [develop Christian] love [that is, learn to unselfishly seek the best for others and to do things for their benefit]. 8 For as these qualities are yours and are increasing [in you as you grow toward spiritual maturity], they will keep you from being useless and unproductive in regard to the true knowledge and greater understanding of our Lord Jesus Christ. 9 For whoever lacks these qualities is blind—shortsighted [closing his spiritual eyes to the truth], having become oblivious to the fact that he was cleansed from his old sins. 10 Therefore, believers, be all the more diligent to make certain about His calling and choosing you [be sure that your behavior reflects and confirms your relationship with God]; for by [f]doing these things [actively developing these virtues], you will never stumble [in your spiritual growth and will live a life that leads others away from sin]; 11 for in this way entry into the eternal kingdom of our Lord and Savior Jesus Christ will be abundantly provided to you.

We must be fruitful and multiply during this lifetime in our walk with God. Paul explains to us even more clearly in *1 Corinthians 2: 7-16* stating:

7But we speak the wisdom of God in a mystery, even the hidden wisdom, which God ordained before the world unto our glory:

8Which none of the princes of this world knew: for had they known it, they would not have crucified the Lord of glory.

9But as it is written, Eye hath not seen, nor ear heard, neither have entered into the heart of man, the things which God hath prepared for them that love him.

10But God hath revealed them unto us by his Spirit: for the Spirit searched all things, yea, the deep things of God.

11For what man knoweth the things of a man, save the spirit of man which is in him? even so the things of God knoweth no man, but the Spirit of God.

12Now we have received, not the spirit of the world, but the spirit which is of God; that we might know the things that are freely given to us of God.

13Which things also we speak, not in the words which man's wisdom teaches, but which the Holy Ghost teaches; comparing spiritual things with spiritual.

14But the natural man receives not the things of the Spirit of God: for they are foolishness unto him: neither can he know them, because they are spiritually discerned.

15But he that is spiritual judges all things, yet he himself is judged of no man.

16For who hath known the mind of the Lord, that he may instruct him? But we have the mind of Christ.

2 Corinthians 4 is the definition of a believer being fruitful and the full description of what being fruitful as a believer looks like. The Passion Translation reads:

1Now, it's because of God's mercy that we have been entrusted with the privilege of this new covenant 'ministry. And we will not quit or faint with weariness. 2We reject every shameful cover-up and refuse to resort to cunning trickery or distorting the Word of God. Instead, we open our souls to you by presenting the truth to everyone's conscience in the sight and presence of God. 3Even if our gospel message is veiled, it is only veiled to those who are perishing, 4for their minds have been blinded by the god of this age, leaving them in unbelief. Their blindness keeps them from seeing the dayspring light of the gospel of the glory of Christ, who is the divine image of God.

5We don't preach us, but rather the lordship of Jesus Christ, for we are your servants for Jesus' sake. 6For God, who said,

"Let brilliant light shine out of darkness,"

is the one who has cascaded his light into us—the brilliant dawning light of the glorious knowledge of God as we gaze into the face of Jesus Christ.

7We are like common clay jars that carry this glorious treasure within, so that this immeasurable power will be seen as God's, not ours. we experience every kind of pressure, we're not crushed. At times we don't know what to do, but quitting is not an option. 9We are persecuted by others, but God has not forsaken us. We may be knocked down, but not out. 10We continually share in the death of Jesus in our own bodies so that the resurrection life of Jesus will be revealed through our humanity. 11We consider living to mean that we are constantly being handed over to death for Jesus' sake so that the life of Jesus will be revealed through our humanity. 12So, then, death is at work in us, but it releases life in you.

13We have the same Spirit of faith that is described in the Scriptures when it says,

"First I believed, then I spoke in faith."

So, we also first believe then speak in faith. 14We do this because we are convinced that he who raised Jesus will raise us up with him, and together we will all be brought into his presence. 15Yes, all things work for your enrichment so that more of God's marvelous grace will spread to more and more people, resulting in an even greater increase of praise to God, bringing him even more glory!

16So no wonder we don't give up. For even though our outer person gradually wears out, our inner being is renewed every single day. 17We view our slight, short-lived troubles in the light of eternity. We see our difficulties as the substance that produces for us an eternal, weighty glory far beyond all comparison, 18because we don't focus our attention on what is seen but on what is unseen. For what is seen is temporary, but the unseen realm is eternal.

As you see in the scriptures we will suffer just as our Savior Jesus Christ did, but we will receive a greater glory than our sufferings in this life when we enter eternity. Not being cut down and cast into the fire should be our desire, and being fruitful, being pruned, and remaining fruitful is the goal. This is the prize for the race we run as believers. Our fruit bearing will produce souls coming into the kingdom of God, joining the church of believers and the Bride of Jesus Christ. We will accept the "Great Commission" that Jesus Christ gave to all who believe in Him:

MATTHEW 28:16-20 (ESV)

The Great Commission

16 Now the eleven disciples went to Galilee, to the mountain to which Jesus had directed them. 17 And when they saw him, they worshiped him, but some doubted. 18 And Jesus came and said to them, "All authority in heaven and on earth has been given to me. 19 Go therefore and make disciples of all nations, baptizing them in[a] the name of the Father and of the Son and of the Holy Spirit, 20 teaching them to observe all that I have commanded you. And behold, I am with you always, to the end of the age."

CHAPTER 8

Building Your House On A Firm Foundation As A Believer-Part I

*I*T IS IMPERATIVE IN the physical world to build your house on a firm foundation. The word foundation is defined in the Oxford Dictionary (2022) as the lowest load-bearing part of a building, typically below ground level, which can be a footing, base substructure, or understructure. It is also defined as an underlying basis or principle, justification, or reason, and lastly, the action of establishing an institution or organization permanently, especially with an endowment (a quality or ability possessed or inherited by someone).

Having a firm foundation when you are building in the natural is very important because of the things the house will have to endure: storms, floods, strong winds, hurricanes, tornados, tsunamis, earthquakes, and fire. This is also true with our spiritual life. The same threats that we have for our physical homes also stands for our spiritual homes.

Matthew 7:24-27 explains this about our spiritual house. It reads:

24 Therefore whosoever heareth these sayings of mine, and doeth them, I will liken him unto a wise man, which built his house upon a rock:

25 And the rain descended, and the floods came, and the winds blew, and beat upon that house; and it fell not: for it was founded upon a rock.

26 And everyone that heareth these sayings of mine, and doeth them not, shall be likened unto a foolish man, which built his house upon the sand:

27 And the rain descended, and the floods came, and the winds blew, and beat upon that house; and it fell: and great was the fall of it.

Point # 1

Hearing the Word and doing the Word enables us to build a firm foundation through Jesus Christ our Lord. It is an act of faith. When we hear, read, or speak the Word, we must believe what we are saying, then our faith is activated and causes us to walk out the Word that we read.

Romans 10:10 (AMP) reads, "For with the heart a person believes [in Christ as Savior] resulting in his justification [that is, being made righteous—being freed of the guilt of sin and made acceptable to God]; and with the mouth he acknowledges and confesses *[his faith openly]*, *resulting in and confirming [his]* *salvation.*"

So, here we find that belief starts in our hearts. We then speak what we are believing by acknowledging and confessing our faith openly. This is hearing and doing. This is the beginning of our foundation being laid.

When a person is born again, the building process begins immediately. Because of the great confession that was made by the new convert, the foundation is being built. God has immediately started the building process in their lives, starting with their foundation.

Point #2

The foundation that is being built upon is the solid foundation, Jesus Christ. Jesus Christ is explaining to the chief priests and Pharisees in *Matthew 21:42-44 which reads, " 42Jesus saith unto them, did ye never read in the scriptures, The stone which the builders rejected, the same is become the head of the corner: this is the Lord's doing, and it is marvelous in our eyes? 43Therefore say I unto you, the kingdom of God shall be taken from you, and given to a nation bringing forth the fruits thereof. 44And whosoever shall fall on this stone shall be broken but on whomsoever it shall fall, it will grind him to powder."*

The Blue Letter Bible Strong's Concordance explains the phrase "shall be broken" as the Greek word pipto (reference

G4,098) and is listed in the Bible a total of 90 times. It is defined as fall, light, or fail. Biblical usage is defined as:

1. to descend from an erect to a prostrate position
a. to fall
i. to be prostrated, fall prostrate
ii. to prostrate oneself
iii. to be removed from power by death

There are also some negative connotations that were given in the definition as well. However, we are focusing on the true meaning of "being broken."

2. The words "grind to powder" in the Blue Letter Bible Strong's concordance is the reference G3,039 and is the Greek word likmao. It sounds like lik-mah-o. This is also a verb and is used in the Bible 2x's. The biblical usage is to winnow or cleanse away the chaff from the grain by winnowing.
3. to scatter
4. to crush to pieces, grind to powder

This is a positive connotation of the words "grind like powder." The Thayer's Greek Lexicon also defines it as:
to winnow, cleanse away the chaff from grain by winnowing (Homer, Xenophon, Plutarch, others; the Sept.).

3. to crush to pieces, grind to powder:

A description of the chaff being cleansed from the grain was when Jesus was adamant when He was speaking about the parable of the Kingdom of heaven in Matthew 13:24-30 which reads:

THE PARABLE OF THE WHEAT AND THE TARES

24 Another parable He put forth to them, saying: "The kingdom of heaven is like a man who sowed good seed in his field; 25 but while men slept, his enemy came and sowed tares among the wheat and went his way. 26 But when the grain had sprouted and produced a crop, then the tares also appeared. 27 So the servants of the owner came and said to him, 'Sir, did you not sow good seed in your field? How then does it have tares?' 28 He said to them, 'An enemy has done this.' The servants said to him, 'Do you want us then to go and gather them up?' 29 But he said, 'No, lest while you gather up the tares you also uproot the wheat with them. 30 Let both grow together until the harvest, and at the time of harvest I will say to the reapers, "First gather together the tares and bind them in bundles to burn them but gather the wheat into my barn."

So, we see here that even as Jesus is explaining to us that being broken (the stone which is Jesus) is good for us but being crushed is bad for us. When you are being crushed, you are a tare that is being cleansed from the wheat and will be bound in bundles and be burned, but the wheat will be gathered by God and be taken into the "barn" which is the Kingdom of heaven.

This revelation written in the Bible about wheat being taken into the barn struck an interest in me as to why it has to be stored in the barn, so I did a little research and found on the website for the Division of Agriculture the reason for storing wheat in the barn is for use later. My God! This is the information I learned.

The goal of wheat drying is to reduce grain moisture content to meet the recommended levels for safe, long-term storage. When placed in storage, wheat should be dried quickly to a moisture level of about 12 percent to minimize any quality deterioration. Wheat drying can be accomplished in bins by blowing large volumes of dry air through the grain. This website will explore the challenges of wheat drying and storage.

However, arguments for on-farm wheat drying include creating a higher quality finished product. Growers realize that when the wheat grain is re-wetted in the field several times while awaiting field drying to dockage levels, the quality is compromised. Therefore, implementing on-farm drying of the freshly harvested wheat will produce higher quality grain. Growers who dry and store their wheat also gain more flexibility in managing their operations and timing of when to sell their wheat.

Wow, so this is showing that the believer (wheat) is cleansed from the tears (unbelievers) when the rock falls on them and crushes them to pieces and grinds them into powder (destroy) so that it will be clean for the Master to use! Hallelujah! The wheat (believers) is broken because they have fallen on the rock of their salvation, which is "Jesus Christ "so that we are in a prostrate position to be used by God.

This excerpt of scripture explains to us that we can allow our foundation to be built on Jesus Christ, our Lord and Savior, and be preserved for the Master's work by falling on the solid rock of our salvation or we won't fall on our foundation Jesus Christ. He will fall on us and crush us to pieces and scatter us.

This is definitely a different perspective of how we are to be careful of how we should build.

I am immediately taken to *1 Corinthians 3:10-15* which reads, *10According to the grace of God which is given unto me, as a wise master builder, I have laid the foundation, and another buildeth thereon. But let every man take heed how he buildeth thereupon.*

11For other foundation can no man lay than that is laid, which is Jesus Christ.

12Now if any man builds upon this foundation gold, silver, precious stones, wood, hay, stubble;

13Every man's work shall be made manifest: for the day shall declare it, because it shall be revealed by fire; and the fire shall try every man's work of what sort it is.

14If any man's work abide which he hath built thereupon, he shall receive a reward.

15If any man's work shall be burned, he shall suffer loss: but he himself shall be saved; yet so as by fire.

This reflects what Jesus was speaking in the Parable of the Kingdom of Heaven, gathering wheat and tares, allowing them to grow up together, and separating them when He is ready to gather them into His barn.

The perpetual picture that is being painted for us as we read the scriptures that have been highlighted is that our foundation can only be built upon Jesus Christ, who is the solid rock of foundation. Everything else will be burned in the fire. We talked last night about being thrown into the fire if we didn't stay connected to Jesus Christ as the Vine and God our Father as the Vine Dresser and producing fruit so we can be pruned. We learned that when our fruit remains, we receive joy in *John Chapter 15:1-8.*

Peter explained to us in 1 *Peter 2:1-5* that Jesus Christ is the Living Stone and that we are lively stones that are building up a spiritual house. *1 Peter 2:1-5* reads, 1 *Wherefore laying aside all malice, and all guile, and hypocrisies, and envies, and all evil speaking's,*

2 As newborn babes, desire the sincere milk of the word, that ye may grow thereby:

3 If so be ye have tasted that the Lord is gracious.

4 To whom coming, as unto a living stone, disallowed indeed of men, but chosen of God, and precious,

5 Ye also, as lively stones, are built up a spiritual house, a holy priesthood, to offer up spiritual sacrifices, acceptable to God by Jesus Christ.

Peter goes on to explain more about the living stone and the lively stones. He says in *1 Peter 2:6-10* the following:

6 Wherefore also it is contained in the scripture, Behold, I lay in Sion a chief corner stone, elect, precious: and he that believeth on him shall not be confounded.

7 Unto you therefore which believe he is precious: but unto them which be disobedient, the stone which the builders disallowed, the same is made the head of the corner,

8 And a stone of stumbling, and a rock of offence, even to them which stumble at the word, being disobedient: whereunto also they were appointed.

9 But ye are a chosen generation, a royal priesthood, a holy nation, a peculiar people; that ye should shew forth the praises of him who hath called you out of darkness into his marvelous light.

10 Which in time past were not a people but are now the people of God: which had not obtained mercy, but now have obtained mercy.

We see again the explanation of being chosen by God through Jesus Christ when He is our solid foundation. This entails us receiving His grace and mercy. When we're in the field planted with the tares, we were in darkness, but now that we have received Jesus Christ and believed on Him, the power of His crucifixion, death, burial, resurrection, ascension and being alive in His mortal body, having taken on immortality and is seated at the right hand of God forever making intercession for us.

This is what "us falling on the rock vs. the rock falling on us" means.

Point #3

How do we know that we are built upon Jesus Christ the Rock of Salvation?

1. We are confirmed by the Holy Spirit that we are children of God.

Romans 8:14-16 reads, "14 For as many as are led by the Spirit of God, they are the sons of God.

15 For ye have not received the spirit of bondage again to fear; but ye have received the Spirit of adoption, whereby we cry, Abba, Father.

16 The Spirit itself beareth witness with our spirit, that we are the children of God:"

2. It is confirmed by our sufferings. If we fall on the stone, we become lively stones from the living stone. Our process is still taking place while we are here on earth. Jesus completed the work that God gave Him and is resting on His throne interceding for us. He is sure to let us know through His Word the benefits of being built up on the solid rock of our salvation.

Romans 8:17-21 reads, "17 And if children, then heirs; heirs of God, and joint heirs with Christ; if so be that we suffer with him, that we may be also glorified together.

18 For I reckon that the sufferings of this present time are not worthy to be compared with the glory which shall be revealed in us.

19 For the earnest expectation of the creature waited for the manifestation of the sons of God.

20 For the creature was made subject to vanity, not willingly, but by reason of him who hath subjected the same in hope,

21 Because the creature itself also shall be delivered from the bondage of corruption into the glorious liberty of the children of God."

We are not only partakers of the good but also the challenges of Jesus Christ. This points us back to *1 Corinthians 3:10-11,* which says *10According to the grace of God which is given unto me, as a wise master builder, I have laid the foundation, and another buildeth thereon. But let every man take heed how he buildeth thereupon.*

11For other foundation can no man lay than that is laid, which is Jesus Christ.

3. The results of our foundation will be revealed when our work is tried according to *1 Corinthians 3:12-15.*

12Now if any man builds upon this foundation gold, silver, precious stones, wood, hay, stubble;

13Every man's work shall be made manifest: for the day shall declare it, because it shall be revealed by fire; and the fire shall try every man's work of what sort it is.

14If any man's work abide which he hath built thereupon, he shall receive a reward.

15If any man's work shall be burned, he shall suffer loss: but he himself shall be saved; yet so as by fire.

The best thing about our work being tried, whether it was good or bad, is that what is good will remain, and what is bad will be destroyed by the fire of God and we will have to build again this time on the foundation of Jesus Christ!

CHAPTER 9

Building Your House On A Firm Foundation As A Believer Part II

I BET YOU'RE ASKING, "WHAT exactly is the foundation of Jesus Christ?" The foundation of Jesus Christ is living your life based upon the (Word of God) Living Word of God. Jesus Christ is the Living Word. Studying the scriptures and doing what the scriptures say is the foundation of Jesus Christ. This is based upon Matthew 7:24-27.

"So, everyone who hears these words of Mine and acts on them, will be like a wise man [a far-sighted, practical, and sensible man] who built his house on the rock. 25 And the rain fell, and the floods and torrents came, and the winds blew and slammed against that house; yet it did not fall, because it had been founded on the rock. 26 And everyone who hears these words of Mine and does not do them, will be like a foolish (stupid) man who built his house on the sand. 27 And the rain fell, and the floods and torrents came, and

the winds blew and slammed against that house; and it fell—and great and complete was its fall."

Doesn't the description in this parable sound familiar? It is familiar with us Falling on the Rock (Jesus Christ) when our house is still standing after the storm ceased. The rock falling on us and crushing us is the example of the foolish man who built his house upon the sand. His house was crushed by the Rock of Salvation because he did not abide in Him.

I wanted to share a testimony of experiencing Jesus Christ being the Solid Rock of my salvation. I explained the other night how I believed that the Lord wanted me to move to Charlotte. It took me three months to be moved into an apartment in Huntersville. The night that I moved in, I was so thankful. As I woke up the next day, I sat up and rubbed my face. The Lord said to me, "Now you will get to know me as Yaweh-Tsuri," which means the Lord your rock! I was overjoyed. But I had no knowledge of the challenges I would face, and how my faith would be tested and tried before I would move to the next place. Yaweh-Tsuri, the Lord our Rock, was first mentioned in *2 Samuel 22:2-4* which reads, *"2 The Lord is my rock, my fortress, and my savior; 3 my God is my rock, in whom I find protection. He is my shield, the power that saves me, and my place of safety. He is my refuge, my savior, the one who saves me from violence. 4 I called on the Lord, who is worthy of praise, and he saved me from my enemies."*

He is also expressed in *Psalms 62:1-2.*

1 The Lord is my rock and my salvation. I wait quietly before God, for my victory comes from him. 2 He alone is my rock and my salvation my fortress where I will never be shaken.

I was able to overcome the challenges I faced because Jesus Christ was my foundation. It was only me and my three sons there. My family lived in towns an hour away, so we were in the place for everyday life alone. I had to trust in God for everything. I gained more knowledge of:

- Who God was and all His attributes
- Who His Son Jesus Christ, my Lord and Savior, is and the different attributes of Him
- A better relationship with the Holy Spirit.

Even as I share this, I'm in awe of the things that God brought me through because of prayer, consecration, worship and being a light in a dark place. I learned what servanthood really was and how to operate in it. I was able to serve in a ministry at a capacity that I never had. I matured in my faith and intercession. My relationship with God is closer now. I also suffered persecution and was being refined by the refiner's fire while I dwelt there for five years. There were many storms and much adversity, but I made it through. I am delighted to say that I made it through! What does this sound like? It sounds like the evidence of being built on the firm foundation, which is our Lord Jesus Christ!

If you put your trust in God, knowing that He is the only one who can truly bring a change in your life, you will be standing

on the firm foundation which is the Word of God, the Living Word, Jesus Christ our Lord, and Savior. Apply the scriptures to your life everyday by faith through your confession, believing in your heart and speaking the Word of God over your life.

CHAPTER 10

The Importance Of Building Your House On The Firm Foundation Part III

IN THE PREVIOUS CHAPTERS, I taught on "How our foundation in Jesus Christ is Built" in many ways.

- by being a hearer of the Word and also a doer of the Word of God.
- That confessing with our mouths the Word of God over our lives and believing in our hearts that the Word of God is true.
- Jesus Christ is the Rock of our Salvation.
- The difference between the wheat and tares.
- The outcome of the Rock (Jesus Christ) when we fall on Him and when He falls on us.
- The difference between falling and being crushed.
- When we are identified by God as wheat, He stores us in His barn for later.

Now we are going to focus on the foundational principle that helps us to build our spiritual house upon Jesus Christ, the Solid Rock of our salvation as a believer.

Matthew 12:46-50 reads, "46While He was still talking to the crowds, it happened that His mother and brothers stood outside, asking to speak to Him. 47Someone said to Him, "Look! Your mother and Your brothers are standing outside asking to speak to You." 48But Jesus replied to the one who told Him, "Who is My mother and who are My brothers?" 49And stretching out His hand toward His disciples [and all His other followers], He said, "Here are My mother and My brothers! 50For [g]whoever does the will of My Father who is in heaven [by believing in Me and following Me] is My brother and sister and mother."

Jesus is showing us here that our foundation is strictly built on "Doing the Will of the Father."

Matthew 7:26 reads, "And everyone that heareth these sayings of mine, and doeth them not, shall be likened unto a foolish man, which built his house upon the sand."

Both scriptures are highlighting the word "Do." Being a doer of the Word of God, which is the will of God, is the only way that you should build your house. In many scriptures throughout the Bible, there are many instances where men and women were instructed to do something to do the will of the Father by God Himself.

Noah: God told him to build the ark because a flood was coming so that he and his family and the animals would be preserved.

Abraham: God instructed him to leave his entire family to go to a land that He would reveal to him.

Moses: The Lord instructed him to speak to the rock so that He could provide water to the children of Israel.

Elijah: The Lord instructed him to go into the mountain and hid him in the cliff of the rock so that He would allow him to see the back of him.

Habakkuk: He prophesied that the Lord would go before His people and lead them into freedom.

Zechariah: He received a word about Zerubbabel concerning him having victory over the great mountain ahead of him being made into a plain.

Jesus Christ: He was crucified for the sins of the people.

There are countless examples of being a hearer and doer of the Word of God.

In James 1:22, we are instructed again to be "doers" of the Word of God so that we will be wise.

James 1:22-25 reads, "22Be doers of the word, and not hearers only. Otherwise, you are deceiving yourselves. 23For anyone who hears the word but does not carry it out is like a man who looks at his face in a mirror, 24and after observing himself goes away and immediately forgets what he looks like. 25But the one who looks intently into the perfect law of freedom and continues to do so—not being a forgetful hearer, but an effective doer—he will be blessed in what he does."

There are things we must do to be in the will of God.

Jesus instructs us in His commandments we must keep doing the will of the Father in Matthew 12:28-31.

THE GREATEST COMMANDMENT

28 One of the teachers of the law came and heard them debating. Noticing that Jesus had given them a good answer, he asked him, "Of all the commandments, which is the most important?"

29 "The most important one," answered Jesus, "is this: 'Hear, O Israel: The Lord our God, the Lord is one.[a] 30 Love the Lord your God with all your heart and with all your soul and with all your mind and with all your strength.'[b] 31 The second is this: 'Love your neighbor as yourself.'[c] There is no commandment greater than these."

In Matthew Chapter 5, there are many instructions that we must do the will of the Father.
1. The beatitudes:
•   being poor in spirit
•   mourning

- being meek
- having a hunger and thirst for righteousness
- being merciful
- being pure in heart
- being peace makers
- persecuted
- blessing our persecutors.

2. not to allow our salt as believers to lose its saltiness
3. being a light to the world, shining without hiding it.
4. practicing and teaching the commands of God
5. not to be a murder
6. getting rid of offense before bringing your gift to the altar.
7. settling matters with those who take you to court in the adversary way
8. not committing adultery
9. divorce and being remarried
10. not taking oaths and swearing
11. treating people the way that we want to be treated
12. and loving your enemies.

Let's study Matthew Chapter 5 so that we understand the Will of the Father. Everything listed in Matthew Chapter 5 requires you to die to yourself and do the Father's will.

None of us want to love people who hurt us and use us despitefully, but God wants us to. We don't want to settle with someone who is taking us to court before seeing the judge. We want to hold grudges when we are offending, and sometimes we want to take the low road instead of the high road by being petty which is not being the light and salt in the earth.

Denying yourself of what we see as "Your Right" to do something goes out of the window when you become a believer of Jesus Christ. We must follow the example of Jesus Christ for Christ to be our Firm Foundation.

In Matthew 16:24-28, Jesus instructs us on "Doing the Will of The Father."

24 Then Jesus said to His disciples, "If anyone desires to come after Me, let him deny himself, and take up his cross, and follow Me. 25 For whoever desires to save his life will lose it, but whoever loses his life for My sake will find it. 26 For what profit is it to a man if he gains the whole world, and loses his own soul? Or what will a man give in exchange for his soul? 27 For the Son of Man will come in the glory of His Father with His angels, and then He will reward each according to his works. 28 Assuredly, I say to you, there are some standing here who shall not taste death till they see the Son of Man coming in His kingdom."

The Apostle Paul explains to the Church of Philippi by using the example of the obedience of Jesus Christ. This is found in Philippians 2:5-8 and reads:

5Let this mind be in you which was also in Christ Jesus:
6Who, existing in the form of God,
did not consider equality with God
something to be grasped, a
7but emptied Himself,
taking the form of a servant,

being made in human likeness.

8And being found in appearance as a man,

He humbled Himself

and became obedient to death—

even death on a cross.

We are also given a similar example that Jesus Christ showed us is also found in 1 Peter 2:21-24 which reads:

21For to this you were called, because Christ also suffered for you, leaving you an example, that you should follow in His footsteps:

22"He committed no sin,

and no deceit was found in His mouth. G

23When they heaped abuse on Him,

He did not retaliate.

when He suffered, He made no threats,

but entrusted Himself to Him who judges justly.

24He Himself bore our sins

in His body on the tree,

so that we might die to sin

and live to righteousness.

"By His stripes you are healed. "

Jesus is our example. Everything He did is written in the Gospel of Jesus Christ and we see Him doing the will of the Father.

In the book of Revelation, we see the judgement of the Lord coming upon the six churches because they were not hearers and doers of the Word of God fully. This starts in Revelation Chapter 2 and is completed in Revelation Chapter 3.

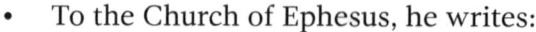

• To the Church of Ephesus, he writes:

2I know your deeds, your labor, and your perseverance. I know that you cannot tolerate those who are evil, and you have tested and exposed as liars those who falsely claim to be apostles. 3Without growing weary, you have persevered and endured many things for the sake of My name.

4But I have this against you: You have abandoned your first love. 5Therefore, keep in mind how far you have fallen. Repent and perform the deeds you did at first. But if you do not repent, I will come to you and remove your lampstand from its place

• to the Church of Smyrna:

9I know your affliction and your poverty—though you are rich! And I am aware of the slander of those who falsely claim to be Jews but are in fact a synagogue of Satan.

10Do not fear what you are about to suffer. Look, the devil is about to throw some of you into prison to test you, and you will suffer tribulation for ten days. Be faithful even unto death, and I will give you the crown of life.

11He who has an ear, let him hear what the Spirit says to the churches. The one who overcomes will not be harmed by the second death

• to the Church of Pergamum

These are the words of the One who holds the sharp, double-edged sword.

13I know where you live, where the throne of Satan sits. Yet you have held fast to My name and have not denied your faith in Me, even in the day when My faithful witness Antipas was killed among

you, where Satan dwells.14But I have a few things against you,
because some of you hold to the teaching of Balaam, who taught
Balak to place a stumbling block before the Israelites so they would
eat food sacrificed to idols and commit sexual immorality. 15In
the same way, some of you also hold to the teaching of the Nicolai-
tans. 16Therefore repent! Otherwise, I will come to you shortly and
wage war against them with the sword of My mouth.

- to the Church of Thyatira

These are the words of the Son of God, whose eyes are like a
blazing fire and whose feet are like polished bronze.

19I know your deeds—your love, your faith, your service, your
perseverance—and your latter deeds are greater than your first.

20But I have this against you: You tolerate that woman Jezebel,
who calls herself a prophetess. By her teaching she misleads My
servants to be sexually immoral and to eat food sacrificed to idols.
21Even though I have given her time to repent of her immorality,
she is unwilling.

22Behold, I will cast her onto a bed of sickness, and those who
commit adultery with her will suffer great tribulation unless they
repent of her deeds. 23Then I will strike her children dead, and all
the churches will know that I am the One who searches minds and
hearts, and I will repay each of you according to your deeds.

24But I say to the rest of you in Thyatira, who do not hold to her
teaching and have not learned the so-called deep things of Satan:
I will place no further burden upon you. 25Nevertheless, hold fast
to what you have until I come. 26And to the one who overcomes
and continues in My work until the end, I will give authority over
the nations. 27He will rule them with an iron scepter and shatter

them like pottery —just as I have received authority from My Father. 28And I will give him the morning star.

29He who has an ear, let him hear what the Spirit says to the churches.

- to the Church of Sardis:

"To the angel of the church in Sardis write:

These are the words of the One who holds the seven Spirits of God and the seven stars.

I know your deeds; you have a reputation for being alive, yet you are dead. 2Wake up and strengthen what remains, which was about to die; for I have found your deeds incomplete in the sight of My God. 3Remember, then, what you have received and heard. Keep it and repent. If you do not wake up, I will come like a thief, and you will not know the hour when I will come upon you.

4But you do have a few people in Sardis who have not soiled their garments, and because they are worthy, they will walk with Me in white. 5Like them, he who overcomes will be dressed in white. And I will never blot out his name from the Book of Life, but I will confess his name before My Father and His angels.

6He who has an ear, let him hear what the Spirit says to the churches.

To the church in Philadelphia:

7To the angel of the church in Philadelphia write:

These are the words of the One who is holy and true, who holds the key of David. What He opens no one can shut, and what He shuts no one can open

8I know your deeds. See, I have placed before you an open door, which no one can shut. For you have only a little strength, yet you have kept My word and have not denied My name. 9Look at those who belong to the synagogue of Satan, who claim to be Jews but are liars instead. I will make them come and bow down at your feet, and they will know that I love you.

10Because you have kept My command to persevere, I will also keep you from the hour of testing that is about to come upon the whole world, to test those who dwell on the earth. 11I am coming soon Hold fast to what you have, so that no one will take your crown. 12The one who overcomes I will make a pillar in the temple of My God, and he will never again leave it. Upon him I will write the name of My God, and the name of the city of My God (the new Jerusalem that comes down out of heaven from My God), and my new name.

13He who has an ear, let him hear what the Spirit says to the churches.

- to the Church of Laodicea

These are the words of the Amen, the faithful and true Witness, the Originator of God's creation.

15I know your deeds; you are neither cold nor hot. How I wish you were one or the other! 16So because you are lukewarm—neither hot nor cold—I am about to vomit you out of My mouth!

17You say, 'I am rich; I have grown wealthy and need nothing.' But you do not realize that you are wretched, pitiful, poor, blind, and naked. 18I counsel you to buy from Me gold refined by fire so that you may become rich, white garments so that you may be clothed, and your shameful nakedness not exposed, and salve to anoint your eyes so that you may see. 19Those I love, I rebuke and discipline. Therefore, be earnest and repent.

20Behold, I stand at the door and knock. If anyone hears My voice and opens the door, I will come in and dine with him, and he *with Me. 21To the one who overcomes, I will grant the right to sit with Me on My throne, just as I overcame and sat down with My Father on His throne.*

22He who has an ear, let him hear what the Spirit says to the churches."

So, we see that there are great consequences if we are not "doers of the Word of God," while being a "hearer and doer of the Word of God" has great rewards.

CHAPTER 11

Why Build Your House On The Firm Foundation Of Jesus Christ Our Lord And Savior Part IV?

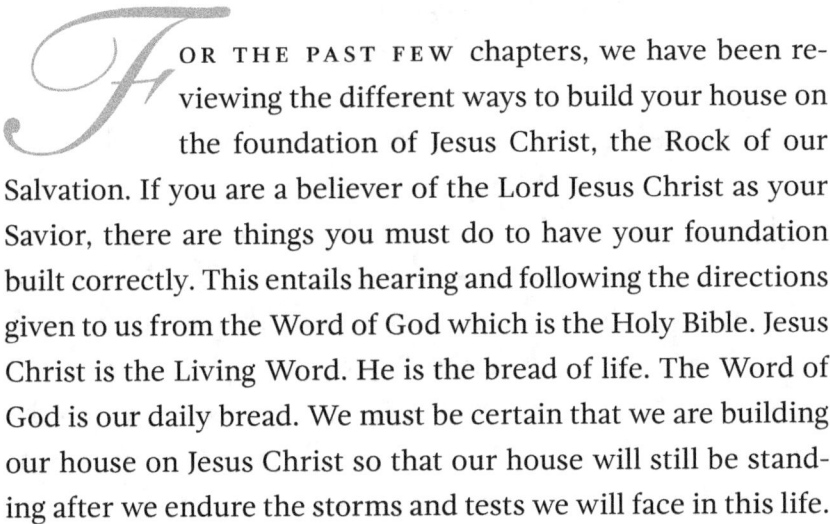

OR THE PAST FEW chapters, we have been re-viewing the different ways to build your house on the foundation of Jesus Christ, the Rock of our Salvation. If you are a believer of the Lord Jesus Christ as your Savior, there are things you must do to have your foundation built correctly. This entails hearing and following the directions given to us from the Word of God which is the Holy Bible. Jesus Christ is the Living Word. He is the bread of life. The Word of God is our daily bread. We must be certain that we are building our house on Jesus Christ so that our house will still be standing after we endure the storms and tests we will face in this life.

James 1:1-4 says, "1 James, a servant of God and of the Lord Jesus Christ, to the twelve tribes which are scattered abroad, greeting. 2 My brethren, count it all joy when ye fall into diver's temptations.3 Knowing this, that the trying of your faith worketh patience.4 But let patience have her perfect work, that ye may be perfect and entire, wanting nothing."

In Part I and Part II, we talked about why we will be persecuted and the results of it.

James 1:12-16

12 Blessed is the man that endures temptation: for when he is tried, he shall receive the crown of life, which the Lord hath promised to them that love him.

13 Let no man say when he is tempted, I am tempted of God: for God cannot be tempted with evil, neither tempted he any man:

14 But every man is tempted, when he is drawn away of his own lust, and enticed.

15 Then when lust hath conceived, it bringeth forth sin: and sin, when it is finished, bringeth forth death.

16 Do not err, my beloved brethren.

We learned in Part I that Jesus was led by the Holy Spirit into the wilderness for forty days. He fasted forty days and forty nights. When His fast was over, the enemy tempted Him in many ways to get him to surrender His Kingship, identity, and power that was given to Him by God the Father. Everything the enemy tried to take from Jesus Christ, our Lord and Savior, was the key to His obedience and finishing the work that God the Father gave Him when He sent him to earth to be the Savior and the Redeemer for our sins. Jesus came to purge away our sins by the shedding of His blood. God was glorified when Jesus Christ, His only Begotten Son, was crucified, died on the cross for our sins, His burial, His resurrection, His ascension, and being seated on the right hand of God forever making intercession for us, the ones who believe on Him.

Jesus was intentional in His pursuit of the Father's will. This is what we call "tunnel vision." According to the Merriam Webster Dictionary, tunnel vision is defined as "constriction of the visual field resulting in loss of peripheral vision" and extreme narrowness of viewpoint such as narrow minded, single-minded, and the concentration on one objective

In Matthew 7:14, Jesus explained to us that straight is the guide and narrow is the way that leads to life and few find it. Peripheral vision is narrow vision. Staying focused on the will of God will ensure that we will gain the incorruptible crown of salvation when we finish the race that the Lord has given to us.

Ecclesiastes 9:11 says that the race is not given to the swift or the battle to the strong, nor does food come to the wise or wealth to the brilliant or favor to the learned, but time and chance happen to them all.

We learned yesterday that "doing the will of the Father" is imperative to our foundation. Doing the will of the Father is called "obedience." The scriptures tell us that Jesus Christ was obedient even unto death.

I have a question for you. Will you be obedient to God the Father even until your death? None of us will be crucified like our Savior was, but we will experience opposition, persecution, hard times, storms, tests, and trials in this life. But do you have your mind made up that you will endure no matter what? Will you trust in God's Word and be a doer of the Word until the day that you die, even when it does not feel good?

Romans 8:37-39
37Nay, in all these things we are more than conquerors through him that loved us.
38For I am persuaded, that neither death, nor life, nor angels, nor principalities, nor powers, nor things present, nor things to come,
39Nor height, nor depth, nor any other creature, shall be able to separate us from the love of God, which is in Christ Jesus our Lord.

Dying to ourselves is a command that was given to us concerning being a follower of Jesus Christ and it is also defined as being a believer. The Bible says if any man will follow Jesus Christ, he must first take up his cross and deny himself daily.

Are you willing to cast down your crown at the feet of Jesus Christ and worship Him with your life by reading the Word and doing what it says?

Jesus says this is how they will know that you are my disciples, by the way that you love one another. This is a call to the Agape love of Jesus Christ! Jesus didn't like what He saw in man, but He still loved man enough to die on the cross for our sins, to be our redeemer, shed His blood for us and to intercede for us forever.

LOVE SHOULD BE THE MOTIVATION OF OUR LIVES

1 Corinthians 13 explains the Love of Jesus Christ.

1If I were to speak with eloquence in earth's many languages, and in the heavenly tongues of angels, yet I didn't express myself with love, my words would be reduced to the hollow sound of nothing more than a clanging cymbal.

2And if I were to have the gift of prophecy with a profound understanding of God's hidden secrets, and if I possessed unending supernatural knowledge, and if I had the greatest gift of faith that could move mountains, but have never learned to love, then I am nothing.

3And if I were to be so generous as to give away everything, I owned to feed the poor, and to offer my body to be burned as a martyr, without the pure motive of love, I would gain nothing of value.

4Love is large and incredibly patient. Love is gentle and consistently kind to all. It refuses to be jealous when blessing comes to someone else. Love does not brag about one's achievements nor inflate its own importance. 5Love does not traffic in shame and disrespect, nor selfishly seek its own honor. Love is not easily irritated or quick to take offense. 6Love joyfully celebrates honesty and finds no delight in what is wrong. 7Love is a safe place of shelter, for it never stops believing the best for others. Love never takes failure as defeat, for it never gives up.

PERFECT LOVE

8Love never stops loving. It extends beyond the gift of prophecy, which eventually fades away. It is more enduring than tongues, which will one day fall silent. Love remains long after words of knowledge are forgotten. 9Our present knowledge and our prophecies are but partial, 10but when love's perfection arrives, the partial will fade away. 11When I was a child, I spoke about childish matters, for I saw things like a child and reasoned like a child. But the day came when I matured, and I set aside my childish ways.

12For now we see but a faint reflection of riddles and mysteries as though reflected in a mirror, but one day we will see face-to-face. My understanding is incomplete now, but one day I will understand everything, just as everything about me has been fully understood. 13Until then, there are three things that remain: faith, hope, and love—yet love surpasses them all. So, above all else, let love be the beautiful prize for which you run.

WALKING IN LOVE TESTIMONY

This is not an easy thing to do, but if you have the help of the Father, you will be able to walk in love the way the Bible instructs us. Matthew chapter 5 is a great help in our walk of love. Walking in love does not always feel good, but it produces wonderful results in our spirits as we walk with God and are obedient to His will, which is the Word of God.

The Bible tells us that love is the bond of perfection. *Colossians 3:12-15 reads," 12 Put on therefore, as the elect of God, holy and beloved, bowels of mercies, kindness, humbleness of mind, meekness, longsuffering; 13Forbearing one another, and forgiving one another, if any man has a quarrel against any: even as Christ forgave you, so also do ye. 14And above all these things put on charity, which is the bond of perfectness. 15And let the peace of*

God rule in your hearts, to the which also ye are called in one body; and be ye thankful."

CHAPTER 12

Psychological Warfare & Overcoming Negative Thoughts

E ALL ARE SUBJECT to psychological warfare as a believer in this lifetime. Apostle Paul taught the church of Ephesus how to overcome the warfare in their minds so that they could do the work of the Lord and be in unity with one another.

> *Ephesians 6:10-20*
> *10 Finally, my brethren, be strong in the Lord, and in the power of his might.*
> *11 Put on the whole armor of God, that ye may be able to stand against the wiles of the devil.*
> *12 For we wrestle not against flesh and blood, but against principalities, against powers, against the rulers of the darkness of this world, against spiritual wickedness in high places.*

13 Wherefore take unto you the whole armor of God, that ye may be able to withstand in the evil day, and having done all, to stand.

14 Stand therefore, having your loins girt about with truth, and having on the breastplate of righteousness.

15 And your feet shod with the preparation of the gospel of peace.

16 Above all, taking the shield of faith, wherewith ye shall be able to quench all the fiery darts of the wicked.

17 And take the helmet of salvation, and the sword of the Spirit, which is the word of God:

18 Praying always with all prayer and supplication in the Spirit and watching thereunto with all perseverance and supplication for all saints.

19 And for me, that utterance may be given unto me, that I may open my mouth boldly, to make known the mystery of the gospel,

20 For which I am an ambassador in bonds: that therein I may speak boldly, as I ought to speak.

The instructions that Paul gave them are clear and easily applicable. How do you apply this scripture to your life you say? Well, you put it in the 1st person. You. When you follow the instructions, you say "I."

Example: "I' put on the full armor of God and so on, until you are finished applying this to your life. The act of recognizing strongholds and vain imaginations is important, but warring against them is necessary.

Proverbs 23:6-8 (AMP)
Do not eat the bread of a selfish man,
Or desire his delicacies;
7
For as he thinks in his heart, so is he [in behavior—one who
manipulates].
He says to you, "Eat and drink,"
Yet his heart is not with you [but it is begrudging the cost].
8
The morsel which you have eaten you will vomit up,
And you will waste your compliments.

These scriptures are saying if we think something about ourselves, we become it in our behavior, and actions. This can also manipulate your emotions.

Your emotions can be deadly. Your emotions may not be the truth in every situation. Emotions come from how we think. Every time we think negative thoughts and do not pull them down and cast down the vain imaginations, it will become a seed that is planted in our hearts. We learned earlier this week that our heart is core of our spirit man. We should not think anything contrary to the word and will of God for our lives.

Paul precedes to instruct the church of Corinth to put on their battle gear: "The full armor of God." The instructions are found in 2 Corinthians 10:1-7.

1Now I Paul myself beseech you by the meekness and gentleness of Christ, who in presence am base among you, but being absent am bold toward you:

2But I beseech you, that I may not be bold when I am present with that confidence, wherewith I think to be bold against some, which think of us as if we walked according to the flesh.

3For though we walk in the flesh, we do not war after the flesh:

4(For the weapons of our warfare are not carnal, but mighty through God to the pulling down of strong holds;)

5Casting down imaginations, and every high thing that exalted itself against the knowledge of God, and bringing into captivity every thought to the obedience of Christ;

6And having in a readiness to revenge all disobedience when your obedience is fulfilled.

7Do ye look on things after the outward appearance? If any man trust to himself that he is Christ's, let him of himself think this again, that, as he is Christ's, even so are we Christ's.

Why do we need to put on the full armor of God? The reason is because no one goes to battle without armor or weapons. Being submitted to God and His Word gives us dominion over the enemy of our souls and minds. If the enemy can find a thought or way of thinking that you have which constantly jeopardizes you or cause you to self-sabotage, he will continue to manipulate your mind through your thoughts. Being sober and vigilant over your spiritual life is important. This message is not entitled about our foundation, but this is a core component of having a firm foundation in Jesus Christ, the Rock of our Salvation.

1 Corinthians 2:12-16

12 Now we have received, not the spirit of the world, but the spirit which is of God; that we might know the things that are freely given to us of God.

13 Which things also we speak, not in the words which man's wisdom teaches, but which the Holy Ghost teaches: comparing spiritual things with spiritual.

14 But the natural man receives not the things of the Spirit of God: for they are foolishness unto him: neither can he know them, because they are spiritually discerned.

15 But he that is spiritual judges all things, yet he himself is judged of no man.

16 For who hath known the mind of the Lord, that he may instruct him? but we have the mind of Christ.

We have been learning according to *Romans 10:10 (AMP)* which reads, " *10 For with the heart a person believes [in Christ as Savior] resulting in his justification [that is, being made righteous—being freed of the guilt of sin and made acceptable to God]; and with the mouth he acknowledges and confesses [his faith openly], resulting in and confirming [his] salvation.*"

So, we see that whatever we believe in our hearts, we acknowledge and confess with our mouths. How we think affects what we believe.

Luke 6:45 (AMP) says, "The [intrinsically] good man produces what is good and honorable and moral out of the good treasure [stored] in his heart; and the [intrinsically] evil man produces *what is wicked and depraved out of the evil [in his heart]; for his mouth speaks from the overflow of his heart."*

The scriptures are constantly showing us the connection between our thoughts, hearts, and mouths. Whatever we have in our hearts will be manifested through our words.

I have two examples. As a believer with strong faith, I know not to speak something that doesn't seem natural to someone who is not spiritual or does not believe at the level I believe or greater. The reason is because their unbelief will plant seeds of doubt into my mind and heart because of the way they think. You cannot rationalize your faith in God with worldly or human wisdom. The Bible is stern. *James 3:13-18* informs us that we can't rely on the wisdom of this world.

James 3:13-18 (AMP)

Who among you is wise and intelligent? Let him by his good conduct show his [good] deeds with the gentleness and humility of true wisdom. 14 But if you have bitter jealousy and selfish ambition in your hearts, do not be arrogant, and [as a result] be in defiance of the truth. 15 This [superficial] wisdom is not that which comes down from above, but is earthly (secular), natural (unspiritual), even demonic. 16 For where jealousy and selfish ambition exist, there is disorder [unrest, rebellion] and every evil thing and morally degrading practice. 17 But the wisdom from above is first pure [morally and spiritually undefiled], then peace-loving [courteous, considerate], gentle, reasonable [and willing to listen], full of compassion and good fruits. It is unwavering, without [self-righteous] hypocrisy [and self-serving guile]. 18 And the seed whose fruit is righteousness (spiritual maturity) is sown in peace by those who make peace [by actively encouraging goodwill between individuals].

This takes us right back to *1 Corinthians 2:16* which reads, *"16 For who hath known the mind of the Lord, that he may instruct him? but we have the mind of Christ."*

I love what the prophet Isaiah told the Lord in *Isaiah 26:1-4* which reads, *"1 In that day shall this song be sung in the land of Judah; We have a strong city; salvation will God appoint for walls and bulwarks.*

2 Open ye the gates, that the righteous nation which kept the truth may enter in.

3 Thou wilt keep him in perfect peace, whose mind is stayed on thee: because he trusted in thee.

4 Trust ye in the LORD forever: for in the LORD JEHOVAH is everlasting strength:"

In the book of Matthew, before Jesus would heal anyone or raise them from the dead, He would remove those who did not have faith in miracles. This is found in *Matthew 9:23-26 which reads,*

"23 When Jesus came to the ruler's house, and saw the flute players [who were professional, hired mourners] and the [grieving] crowd making an uproar, 24 He said, "Go away; for the girl is not dead, but is sleeping." And they laughed and jeered at Him. 25 But when the crowd had been sent outside, Jesus went in and took her by the hand, and the girl got up. 26 And the news about this spread throughout all that district."

So, we must be like Jesus, pulling down every imagination that exalts itself against the knowledge of Jesus Christ! Unbelief and doubt are a way of thinking.

Doubt is defined in the Oxford Dictionary (2022) as: noun
1.   a feeling of uncertainty or lack of conviction:
"Some doubt has been cast upon the authenticity of this account." "They had doubts that they would ever win."

Unbelief is defined as:
1.   lack of religious belief; an absence of faith:
"The darkness of unbelief." "The distinction between doubt and unbelief is valid and useful."

These are things that exalt themselves higher than the knowledge of Jesus Christ! This is because the Bible says that God has given us ALL THINGS that pertain unto life and godliness through the Knowledge of Jesus Christ in *2 Peter 1:3 (NIV) which reads, "His divine power has given us everything we need for a godly life through our knowledge of him who called us by his own glory and goodness."*

The Bible says, "Anything that is not of faith is a sin and it is impossible to please God without faith." Faith is a way of thinking, believing, and speaking (confessing).

The second example are thoughts that constantly plague your mind that are negative. They are usually thoughts about yourself or other people. These thoughts come from offense and unforgiveness. It is also a sign of demonic oppression.

Proverbs 23:6-8
6 Do not eat the bread of a selfish man,
Or desire his delicacies;
7
For as he thinks in his heart, so is he [in behavior—one who manipulates].
He says to you, "Eat and drink,"
Yet his heart is not with you [but it is begrudging the cost].
8
The morsel which you have eaten you will vomit up,
And you will waste your compliments.

Whatever 'WE" think in our hearts (spirit), so are we. This will be revealed in our behavior.

People who think less of themselves than what the Word of God says about them is because they believe something that has been said about them or an act that was committed against them where they took offense or believed that was not true about them.

I call these thoughts intrusive. They come to set up barriers and walls in our minds and skew our perceptions. It is important when these thoughts come to recognize them immediately and to cast them down. They come with an imagination. The imagination is usually a picture in your mind of the event that took place or a feeling you felt when something happened, whether you took an offense or not.

According to WebMD, an intrusive thought is an unwelcome, involuntary thought, image, or unpleasant idea that may become an obsession, is upsetting or distressing, and can feel difficult to manage or eliminate. These thoughts produce anxiety, depression, or obsessive-compulsive disorder (OCD).

Some examples of intrusive thoughts include:
- Sexual thoughts
- Violent thoughts
- negative thoughts
- Bizarre
- weird
- or paranoid thoughts.

Isaiah 26:1-4

1 In that day shall this song be sung in the land of Judah; We have a strong city; salvation will God appoint for walls and bulwarks.

2 Open ye the gates, that the righteous nation which kept the truth may enter in.

3 Thou wilt keep him in perfect peace, whose mind is stayed on thee: because he trusted in thee.

4 Trust ye in the LORD forever: for in the LORD JEHOVAH is everlasting strength:

So, we see here keeping our minds on the Lord Jehovah, we will have everlasting peace and he will be our strength during this battle in our thought lives.

Psalms 119:165 says, "Great peace have those who love your law; nothing can make them stumble."

When we continue to study the Word of God, it will cause us to have an understanding heart and ears to hear, so that we will come to God, and He can heal us. Being wounded or having wounds that have never healed is an open door to offense. When we seek God for healing in our souls or inner healing, the Lord will begin to reveal the areas of our lives where we are stuck. Offense does not let you move on. It keeps you in the same place where the offense took place spiritually, just like if you were standing on a sidewalk where they were pouring concrete. If you do not get out before it starts drying, you may remain there permanently. This is psychological warfare. The only weapon that is strong enough to remove you from this entanglement is speaking the Word of God over your mind and heart and making confessions.

When you combat every thought that is trying to exalt itself in your life higher than the knowledge of the Lord Jesus Christ, which is how we receive and obtain all things that pertain unto life and godliness, you begin to experience freedom and the bondages in your mind will begin to break.

Hebrews 4:12-13

12 For the word of God is quick and powerful, and sharper than any two-edged sword, piercing even to the dividing asunder of soul and spirit, and of the joints and marrow, and is a discerner of the thoughts and intents of the heart.

13 Neither is there any creature that is not manifest in his sight: but all things are naked and opened unto the eyes of him with whom we must do.

Pulling down strong holds in our minds and casting down imaginations, bringing your thoughts into the obedience of Jesus Christ by speaking the Word of God in opposition to your thoughts will cause you to have the victory over the enemy.

PSYCHOLOGICAL WARFARE AND NEGATIVE THOUGHTS TESTIMONY

So, during my journey as a believer in Jesus Christ, I have experienced much opposition from the enemy as all believers do!. I have been called names, mistreated and so on. However, these things once formed a strong hold in my mind because I was offended and didn't forgive the person right away. My silence during these attacks on my character and spiritual identity caused me more inner turmoil, which changed my perspective of people, employers, coworkers, people in churches or those who say they are "saved."

The Lord led me one morning as I was praying to Isaiah 11:1-5 and I read it. This is a prophecy about Jesus Christ.

11 And there shall come forth a rod out of the stem of Jesse, and a Branch shall grow out of his roots:

2 And the spirit of the LORD shall rest upon him, the spirit of wisdom and understanding, the spirit of counsel and might, the spirit of knowledge and of the fear of the LORD.

3 And shall make him of quick understanding in the fear of the LORD: and he shall not judge after the sight of his eyes, neither reprove after the hearing of his ears:

4 But with righteousness shall he judge the poor and reprove with equity for the meek of the earth: and he shall smite the earth: with the rod of his mouth, and with the breath of his lips shall he slay the wicked.

5 And righteousness shall be the girdle of his loins, and faithfulness the girdle of his reins.

I began to apply these scriptures to my life. 1 John 4:17 says as Jesus was in this world, so are we in this world. I began to speak both scriptures over my life daily.

I noticed my confidence returning, and I didn't act according to the accusations. This was God affirming me of who I was. The Word of God took my thoughts captive and caused them to be obedient to the Lord Jesus Christ in my life.

The Lord also directed me to Romans 8:28-30. The Berean Study Bible (BSB) translation reads:

28And we know that God works all things together for the good of those who love Him, who are called according to His purpose. 29For those God foreknew, He also predestined to be conformed to the image of His Son, so that He would be the firstborn among many brothers. 30And those He predestined, He also called; those He called, He also justified; those He justified, He also glorified.

This was God confirming my identity again. The more I stand on these scriptures, the less I think about the opposition I face. I am determined not to allow things from my past or present to constrain me or hold me back and cause me to digress spiritually.

In this teaching, I revealed strategies on overcoming the psychological warfare that we as believers face every day.

Remember, any thought that causes fear, pride, anger, hatred, rage, depression, anxiety, keeps you in your past, or evil imaginations are not from God. They need to be cast down or pulled down and brought into the obedience of the Lord Jesus Christ while invoking revenge when your obedience is fulfilled.

CHAPTER 13

Boasting in the Lord

T IS VERY IMPORTANT as a believer in Jesus Christ that we give God the Glory for everything He does in our lives. For we know that without God, we can do nothing. He is the one who causes the moon to rise, the sun to shine, and the stars to shine. All things were made by Him and through Him. God is the creator of the universe, the stars, the skies, the moon, and the sun.

That is why it is important that we glorify God in all things. The moon, sun, stars, or the earth cannot do anything for mankind. In the beginning after God was finished building the earth, He saw everything as good. God said after He created man, that we will have dominion over everything that He created. From the creeping things, animals, the production from the ground and the trees. God made all things for us so that we could be fruitful and multiply.

There are countless and numerous times in the Bible, where men and women of God, tribes and groups worshipped the Lord and boasted in Him to give Him the glory for their victories. It is important to return honor to whom it is due. *Proverbs 3:27* which says, *"Do not withhold good from those to whom it is due, when it is in your power to act. If you have the power to do good, do it as unto the Lord. God bless and do tell the Lord thank you."*

When we worship and honor the Lord in our afflictions, sufferings, persecution, accomplishments, and achievements, we are saying to God, this could not happen without your hand moving in my life. This could not happen:

- If you didn't show up for me.
- If your grace and mercy were not with me.
- If you left me and forsook me.
- If you didn't answer my prayers.
- If you didn't bring this person or that person into my life.

Giving honor to God by boasting in Him is the key to perpetual blessings. The blessings come from our obedience and recognizing who God is!

Isaiah 43:1-28

43 But now thus saith the LORD that created thee, O Jacob, and he that formed thee, O Israel, Fear not: for I have redeemed thee, I have called thee by thy name; thou art mine.

2 When thou pass through the waters, I will be with thee; and through the rivers, they shall not overflow thee: when thou walk through the fire, thou shalt not be burned; neither shall the flame kindle upon thee.

3 For I am the LORD thy God, the Holy One of Israel, thy Savior: I gave Egypt for thy ransom, Ethiopia and Seba for thee.

4 Since thou were precious in my sight, thou hast been honorable, and I have loved thee: therefore, will I give men for thee, and people for thy life.

5 Fear not: for I am with thee: I will bring thy seed from the east and gather thee from the west.

6 I will say to the north, give up; and to the south, keep not back: bring my sons from far, and my daughters from the ends of the earth.

7 Even every one that is called by my name: for I have created him for my glory, I have formed him; yea, I have made him.

8 Bring forth the blind people that have eyes, and the deaf that have ears.

9 Let all the nations be gathered, and let the people be assembled: who among them can declare this and shew us former things? let them bring forth their witnesses, that they may be justified: or let them hear, and say, it is truth.

10 Ye are my witnesses, saith the LORD, and my servant whom I have chosen: that ye may know and believe me and understand that I am he: before me there was no God formed, neither shall there be after me.

11 I, even I, am the LORD; and beside me there is no savior.

12 I have declared, and have saved, and I have shewed, when there was no strange god among you: therefore, ye are my witnesses, saith the LORD, that I am God.

13 Yea, before the day was, I am he; and there is none that can deliver out of my hand: I will work, and who shall let it?

14 Thus saith the LORD, your redeemer, the Holy One of Israel; For your sake I have sent to Babylon, and have brought down all their nobles, and the Chaldeans, whose cry is in the ships.

15 I am the LORD, your Holy One, the creator of Israel, your King.

16 Thus saith the LORD, which makes a way in the sea, and a path in the mighty waters.

17 Which bringeth forth the chariot and horse, the army, and the power; they shall lie down together, they shall not rise: they are extinct, they are quenched as tow.

18 Remember ye not the former things, neither consider the things of old.

19 Behold, I will do a new thing; now it shall spring forth; shall ye not know it? I will even make a way in the wilderness, and rivers in the desert.

20 The beast of the field shall honor me, the dragons, and the owls: because I give waters in the wilderness, and rivers in the desert, to give drink to my people, my chosen.

21 This people have I formed for myself; they shall shew forth my praise.

22 But thou hast not called upon me, O Jacob; but thou hast been weary of me, O Israel.

23 Thou hast not brought me the small cattle of thy burnt offerings; neither hast thou honored me with thy sacrifices. I have not caused thee to serve with an offering, nor wearied thee with incense.

24 Thou hast bought me no sweet cane with money, neither hast thou filled me with the fat of thy sacrifices: but thou hast made me to serve with thy sins, thou hast wearied me with thine iniquities.

25 I, even I, am he that blotted out thy transgressions for mine own sake and will not remember thy sins.

26 Put me in remembrance: let us plead together: declare thou, that thou mayest be justified.

27 Thy first father hath sinned, and thy teachers have trans-gressed against me.

28 Therefore I have profaned the princes of the sanctuary, and have given Jacob to the curse, and Israel to reproaches.

God is the one who causes all things to work together for the good of those who love the Lord and are called according to His purpose.

When we are operating in the divine will of God, we will be able to see more clearly how God is at work in our lives, even when things look like they are contrary to what God has spoken concerning you!

God is the Almighty God! Everything begins with Him, and everything ends with Him. *John 1: 1-3 reads, "1 In the beginning was the Word, and the Word was with God, and the Word was God. 2 The same was in the beginning with God. 3 All things were made by him; and without him was not anything made that was made."*

Colossians 1:23-29

23 If ye continue in the faith grounded and settled and be not moved away from the hope of the gospel, which ye have heard, and which was preached to every creature which is under heaven; whereof I Paul am made a minister.

24 Who now rejoice in my sufferings for you, and fill up that which is behind of the afflictions of Christ in my flesh for his body's sake, which is the church:

25 Whereof I am made a minister, according to the dispensation of God, which is given to me for you, to fulfil the word of God.

26 Even the mystery which hath been hid from ages and from generations, but now is made manifest to his saints:

27 To whom God would make known what the riches of the glory of this mystery is among the Gentiles, which is Christ in you, the hope of glory:

28 Whom we preach, warning every man, and teaching every man in all wisdom; that we may present every man perfect in Christ Jesus:

29 Whereunto I also labor, striving according to his working, which worketh in me mightily.

Continuing to boast in the Lord is bringing Him glory and giving Him permission to continue to fight on your behalf and to bless you! Here are a few scriptures on boasting in the Lord:

Psalms 84:11-12

11 For the LORD God is a sun and shield: the LORD will give grace and glory: no good thing will he withhold from them that walk uprightly.

12 O LORD of hosts blessed is the man that trusted in thee.

Psalms 34:1-3

1 I will always bless the LORD:

His praise shall continually be in my mouth.

2 My soul shall make her boast in the LORD:

The humble shall hear thereof and be glad.

3 O magnify the LORD with me,

And let us exalt his name together.

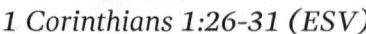

1 Corinthians 1:26-31 (ESV)

26 For consider your calling, brothers: not many of you were wise according to worldly standards,[a] not many were powerful, not many were of noble birth. 27 But God chose what is foolish in the world to shame the wise; God chose what is weak in the world to shame the strong; 28 God chose what is low and despised in the world, even things that are not, to bring to nothing things that are, 29 so that no human being[b] might boast in the presence of God. 30 And because of him[c] you are in Christ Jesus, who became to us wisdom from God, righteousness and sanctification and redemption, 31 so that, as it is written, "Let the one who boasts, boast in the Lord."

2 Corinthians 11:30 (ESV)

30 If I must boast, I will boast of the things that show my weakness. 31 The God and Father of the Lord Jesus, the who is blessed forever, knows that I am not lying. 32 At Damascus, the governor under King Aretas was guarding the city of Damascus to seize me, 33 but I was let down in a basket through a window in the wall and escaped his hands.

2 Corinthians 10:13-17

13 But we will not boast beyond limits, but will boast only with regard to the area of influence God assigned to us, to reach even to you. 14 For we are not overextending ourselves, as though we did not reach you, for we were the first to come all the way to you with the gospel of Christ. 15 We do not boast beyond limit in the labors of others. But our hope is that as your faith increases, our area of influence among you may be greatly enlarged, 16 so that we may preach the gospel in lands beyond you, without boasting of work already done in another's area of influence. 17 "Let the one who boasts, boast in the Lord." 18 For it is not the one who commends himself who is approved, but the one whom the Lord commends.

Exodus 15:20-27

20 Then Miriam the prophetess, the sister of Aaron [and Moses], took a timbrel in her hand, and all the women followed her with timbrels and dancing. 21 Miriam answered them,

"Sing to the LORD, for He has triumphed gloriously and is highly exalted;

The horse and its rider He has hurled into the sea."

The LORD Provides Water

22 Then Moses led Israel from the Red Sea, and they went into the Wilderness of Shur; they went [a distance of] three days (about thirty-three miles) in the wilderness and found no water. 23 Then they came to Marah, but they could not drink its waters because they were [d]bitter; therefore it was named Marah (bitter). 24 The people [grew discontented and] grumbled at Moses, saying, "What are we going to drink?" 25 Then he cried to the LORD [for help], and the LORD showed him a tree, [a branch of] which he threw into the waters, and the waters became sweet.

There the LORD made a statute and an ordinance for them, and there [e]He tested them, 26 saying, "If you will diligently listen and pay attention to the voice of the LORD your God, and do what is right in His sight, and listen to His commandments, and keep [foremost in your thoughts and actively obey] all His precepts and statutes, then I will not put on you any of the diseases which I have put on the Egyptians; for I am the [f]LORD who heals you."

27 Then the children of Israel came to Elim where there were twelve springs of water and seventy date palms, and they camped there beside the waters.

THE RESULTS WE RECEIVE WHEN WE BOAST IN THE LORD

There are countless times in every book of the Bible where the people of God may have been afflicted, oppressed, or persecuted. Yet they did not boast about being afflicted. They boasted in the Lord God almighty: the one who was their keeper, their God, their defender, and their warrior.

Even Job continued to boast in the Lord during his sufferings and afflictions after the Lord gave the enemy permission to touch his life but not to take his life. Job never once gave up on God. He did see his afflictions as something that was placed upon him by God, but he made it clear that he still trusted in God. This is very important in every believer's life, especially when we don't understand our situations and circumstances and why we are going through something. Job's friends even thought that Job had committed sin in the sight of the Lord. Job stayed focused on God. He was even broken down to the point that he just waited on God to change his life. He listened to his friends accuse him of being in sin because of his sufferings. However, what the enemy did not know was that even God had a hedge of protection around Job before he received the Lord's approval to attack him. Job was considered the most righteous man (blameless, upright, feared God, and turned away from evil) in the land. Job would even rise early in the morning and offer burnt offerings to God for all his children if they sinned against God while they were partying during the night. Job did this continually. This is found in Job 1:1-5. Because of Job's love and fear for God, Job knew God. He spent time in God's presence and was close to God. The enemy didn't know this. He only knew that God had a hedge of protection around him that was impenetrable.

Job showed us in this passage how to be seen as blameless, upright, having the fear of God, and turning away from evil is beneficial to us. We must have clean hands and pure hearts unto God.

Job ended up boasting in the Lord after he received new blessings from God for his repentance and faithfulness to God.

Job 42: 12-17

12 So the LORD blessed the latter end of Job more than his beginning: for he had fourteen thousand sheep, and six thousand camels, and a thousand yoke of oxen, and a thousand she asses.

13 He had also seven sons and three daughters.

14 And he called the name of the first, Jemima; and the name of the second, Kezia; and the name of the third, Kerenhappuch.

15 And in all the land were no women found so far as the daughters of Job: and their father gave them inheritance among their brethren.

16 After this lived Job a hundred and forty years, and saw his sons, and his sons' sons, even four generations.

17 So Job died, being old and full of days.

It is very important to boast and glory in the Lord in your afflictions and blessings. Suffering, afflictions, and blessings are the epitome of a believer's life. We will go through it, but we will not be vain in our glory. Our glory should always be unto the Lord, knowing that He is our rewarder.

CHAPTER 14

The Importance of Repentance

N O ONE WANTS TO hear teaching or preaching
on sin. Did you know that sin is the root cause
of the fall of believers/followers of Christ? Sin
starts with temptation. Once the temptation enters your heart,
it creates a desire for sin which is also called "lust." When the
lust takes us over, then we commit the sin, and when we commit the sin, it causes us to die spiritually. This is found in James
1:13-15.

James 1:13-15
*13 Let no one say when he is tempted, "I am being tempted by
God," for God cannot be tempted with evil, and he himself tempts
no one. 14 But each person is tempted when he is lured and enticed
by his own desire. 15 Then desire when it has conceived gives birth
to sin, and sin when it is fully grown brings forth death.*

The Bible is very clear in *Romans 6:23 which reads, "The
wage of sin is death, but the gift of God is eternal life.".*

Romans 6:20-23 (ESV)

20 For when you were slaves of sin, you were free regarding righteousness. 21 But what fruit were you getting at that time from the things of which you are now ashamed? For the end of those things is death. 22 But now that you have been set free from sin and have become slaves of God, the fruit you get leads to sanctification and its end, eternal life. 23 For the wages of sin is death, but the gift of God is eternal life in Christ Jesus our Lord.

Matthew 6:22-24 (ESV)

22 "The eye is the lamp of the body. So, if your eye is healthy, your whole body will be full of light, 23 but if your eye is bad, your whole body will be full of darkness. If then the light in you is darkness, how great is the darkness!

24 "No one can serve two masters, for either he will hate the one and love the other, or he will be devoted to the one and despise the other. You cannot serve God and money.

We must keep our eyes healthy by being single (looking in one direction-Jesus Christ, The word of God, God, and the Holy Spirit). Keep the darkness out of our eyes: the lust of the flesh, the lust of the eye, and the pride of life.

1 John 2:15-17 (ESV)

15 Do not love the world or the things in the world. If anyone loves the world, the love of the Father is not in him. 16 For all that is in the world—the desires of the flesh and the desires of the eyes and pride of life—is not from the Father but is from the world. 17 And the world is passing away along with its desires, but whoever does the will of God abides forever.

What exactly are the desires of the flesh?

Galatians 5: 19-21
19 Now the works of the flesh are evident: sexual immorality, impurity, sensuality, 20 idolatry, sorcery, enmity, strife, jealousy, fits of anger, rivalries, dissensions, divisions, 21 envy,4 drunkenness, orgies, and things like these. I warn you, as I warned you before, that those who do5 such things will not inherit the kingdom of God.

Paul is warning us prior to listing the desires of the flesh in *Galatians 5:16-18.*
16 But I say, walk by the Spirit, and you will not gratify the desires of the flesh. 17 For the desires of the flesh are against the Spirit, and the desires of the Spirit are against the flesh, for these are opposed to each other, to keep you from doing the things you want to do. 18 But if you are led by the Spirit, you are not under the law.

What is the lust of the eye?

According to Christianity.com, the lust of the eyes can be described as the sinful desire to want to have the things we see, such as money, material possessions, houses, cars, a certain physical appearance, or even looking at someone lustfully. Our eyes see everything physical around us and our own eyes can cause us to covet or want something we do not possess.

The lust of the eye is basically covetousness, which means to desire something that you see someone else with, something that does not belong to you, or something that is of worldly value that can cause you to worship or commit idolatry to it and against God.

What is the pride of life?

It's when the sin of being arrogant or boastful about what one has or has achieved. It is also the sin of seeing others as inferior because of your achievements, personality, or status. Examples are self-righteousness or feeling more righteous than others, feeling more important than others on the account of your beauty, fame, etc.

Everyone sins and or has sinned. Let me prove it to you!

1 John 1:5-10
5 This is the message [of God's promised revelation] which we have heard from Him and now announce to you, that God is Light [He is holy, His message is truthful, He is perfect in righteousness], and in Him there is no darkness at all [no sin, no wickedness, no imperfection]. 6 If we say that we have fellowship with Him and yet walk in the darkness [of sin], we lie and do not practice the truth; 7 but if we [really] walk in the Light [that is, live each and every day in conformity with the precepts of God], as He Himself is in the Light, we have [true, unbroken] fellowship with one another [He with us, and we with Him], and the blood of Jesus His Son cleanses us from all sin [by erasing the stain of sin, keeping us cleansed from sin in all its forms and manifestations]. 8 If

we say we have no sin [refusing to admit that we are sinners], we delude ourselves and the truth is not in us. [His word does not live in our hearts.] 9 If we [freely] admit that we have sinned and confess our sins, He is faithful and just [true to His own nature and promises] and will forgive our sins and cleanse us continually from all unrighteousness [our wrongdoing, everything not in conformity with His will and purpose]. 10 If we say that we have not sinned [refusing to admit acts of sin], we make Him [out to be] a liar [by contradicting Him] and His word is not in us.

This is proof that we all sin and have sinned and need forgiveness.

When John the Baptist was baptizing the people to get them ready for Jesus Christ, he warned those who came to be baptized by him, who were sinning, and they knew better: This is what he said in *Luke 3:7-9.*

7 So he began saying to the crowds who were coming out to be baptized by him, "You brood of [f]vipers, who warned you to flee from the wrath [of God that is] to come? 8 Therefore produce fruit that is worthy of [and consistent with your] repentance [that is, live changed lives, turn from sin and seek God and His righteousness]. And do not even begin to say to yourselves [as a defense], 'We have Abraham for our father [and so our heritage assures us of salvation]'; for I say to you that from these stones God is able to raise up children (descendants) for Abraham [for God can replace the unrepentant, regardless of their heritage, with those who are obedient]. 9 Even now the axe [of God's judgment] is swinging to-

ward the root of the trees; so, every tree that does not produce good fruit is being cut down and thrown into the fire."

Let's go over the sins listed in the Bible.

Proverbs 6:16-19 says, "These six things the LORD hates; Indeed, seven are repulsive to Him:17 A proud look [the attitude that makes one overestimate oneself and discount others], a lying tongue, and hands that shed innocent blood, 18 A heart that creates wicked plans, Feet that run swiftly to evil,19 A false witness who breathes out lies [even half-truths], And one who spreads discord (rumors) among brothers."

Here is a list of sins that we must get rid in of our lives:
- Lying
- Hatred
- Unforgiveness
- Slander
- Gossiping
- Being a busy body
- Causing strife
- Causing someone to fall into sin
- Having evil desires in your heart towards someone and acting otherwise
- False accusations
- Blaspheming the holy spirit
- Homosexuality
- Bestiality
- Doing things without faith
- Not being sure of your salvation

- Perversion
- Stealing
- Manipulation
- God desires obedience and not sacrifice.
- Fornication
- Adultery
- Lust
- Disobedient

KING SAUL WAS DISOBEDIENT TO GOD

1 Samuel 15:17-23

17 And Samuel said, "Though you are little in your own eyes, are you not the head of the tribes of Israel? The LORD anointed you king over Israel. 18 And the LORD sent you on a mission and said, 'Go, devote to destruction the sinners, the Amalekites, and fight against them until they are consumed.' 19 Why then did you not obey the voice of the LORD? Why did you pounce on the spoil and do what was evil in the sight of the LORD?" 20 And Saul said to Samuel, "I have obeyed the voice of the LORD. I have gone on the mission on which the LORD sent me. I have brought Agag the king of Amalek, and I have devoted the Amalekites to destruction. 21 But the people took of the spoil, sheep and oxen, the best of the things devoted to destruction, to sacrifice to the LORD your God in Gilgal." 22 And Samuel said, "Has the LORD as great delight in burnt offerings and sacrifices, as in obeying the voice of the LORD? Behold, to obey is better than sacrifice, and to listen than the fat of rams. 23 For rebellion is as the sin of divination, and presumption is as iniquity and idolatry. Because you have rejected the word of the LORD, he has also rejected you from being king."

We must make sure that we get rid of the sin in our lives and that we are obedient to God so that we won't be rejected by Him. We must always seek the forgiveness and acceptance of God more than anything else in this life!

I pray this book was able to give you insight on the life of being a believeras you embrace your new life in Jesus Christ, our Lord and Savior.I pray that your walk with the Lord is everlasting and that you are able to run the race that has been set before you with patience, as you look diligently unto Jesus Christ our Lord and Savior! Grace and peace be unto you and may the blessings of the Lord be upon you for the rest of your days in Jesus Name. Amen.

About The Author

NIKEYA QUICK HAS THREE wonderful sons. She is a woman of faith and an author. Her endless pursuit of Jesus Christ and having a heart for God helps her complete the assignment on her life.

Her passion for the new believer and those who are backslidden are consistent with the word of God. She ministers salvation to those who are lost while she shops and attends events by the leading of the Holy Spirit in certain areas of her region.

She is a partner at a Bible-based ministry in Charlotte, NC, and is accountable to her leaders. She is an encourager to others and will intercede for them in order to see them fulfill the purpose and destiny that God created for them. Her utmost desire is to see the body of Christ in unity, as it speaks of in Ephesians 4:1-13.

She is also the author of Walking Into Your Destiny by Faith.

Index

forgive, 103, 121
foundation, 15, 38, 42, 58, 59, 60, 64, 65, 66, 68, 69, 71, 72, 73, 74, 85, 87, 95
friendship, 5, 9
fruit, 2, 6, 19, 46, 47, 48, 49, 51, 52, 56, 65, 97, 118, 121, 122
Fruitlessness, 51

G

Gethsemane, 8
glory, 12, 15, 31, 32, 33, 46, 51, 53, 54, 55, 56, 67, 78, 99, 106, 108, 111, 116
God, 1, 3, 4, 5, 6, 8, 9, 12, 13, 14, 15, 16, 17, 19, 20, 21, 22, 23, 24, 25, 26, 27, 28, 30, 31, 32, 33, 34, 35, 36, 37, 38, 39, 40, 41, 42, 43, 44, 45, 46, 47, 48, 49, 50, 51, 53, 54, 55, 56, 59, 60, 62, 63, 64, 65, 66, 67, 68, 69, 70, 71, 72, 73, 74, 75, 76, 77, 78, 79, 81, 82, 83, 84, 85, 86, 87, 88, 89, 90, 91, 92, 93, 94, 95, 96, 97, 98, 99, 100, 101, 102, 103, 104, 105, 106, 107, 108, 110, 111, 112, 113, 114, 115, 117, 118, 119, 120, 121, 123, 124, 125
good, 2, 5, 6, 10, 11, 13, 22, 26, 32, 34, 40, 46, 51, 52, 62, 68, 76, 88, 90, 96, 97, 104, 106, 107, 110, 111, 122
Gossiping, 122
grace, 15, 43, 56, 64, 66, 68, 107, 111
Great Commission, 56, 57
Greek, 23, 36, 43, 60, 61

H

Habakkuk, 75
happy, 12

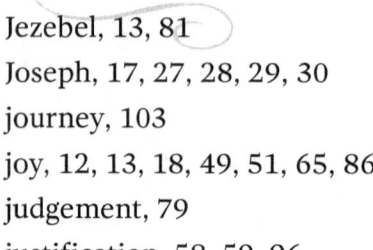

mediocre, 2

Messiah, 22, 29

mind, 9, 27, 37, 49, 51, 54, 76, 78, 80, 88, 90, 95, 96, 97, 98, 99, 100, 101, 102, 103

mission, 2, 123

money, 41, 42, 109, 118, 119

Moses, 21, 22, 75, 113

motives, 6, 9

Mount Moriah, 21

mountain, 20, 21, 22, 26, 39, 57, 75

N

negative thoughts, 94, 101

Noah, 15, 16, 75

O

obsession, 101

offense, 77, 89, 100, 101, 102

opposition, 1, 44, 87, 103, 105

oppressed, 38, 114

overcome, 2, 14, 26, 71, 92

P

paranoia, 5

paranoid thoughts, 101

passion, 125

patience, 13, 86, 124

R